FINDING
YOUR VOICE
IN THE ROOM

I0458031

Dr. Byram McKinzie, Sr.

WWW.TRUEVINEPUBLISHING.ORG

Finding Your Voice in the room
Dr. Byram McKinzie, Sr.

Published by
True Vine Publishing Company
810 Dominican Dr.
Nashville TN 37228
www.TrueVinePublishing.org

ISBN: 978-1-968092-28-3 Paperback
ISBN: 978-1-968092-30-6 eBook

Printed in the United States of America.
For information, contact the author.

DEDICATION

This book is dedicated to people who are seeking to reclaim their voice after being silenced by years of narcissistic abuse. Your voice matters.

ACKNOWLEDGEMENT

I thank the cosmic birther of truth who helped me realize I needed to experience personal growth. I thank my favorite person in the world; my wife Latoya. I thank my children and family who supported me on this journey to complete this book. I thank the friends and associates who helped shape the framework for this book. I thank those who meant it for evil while the cosmic birther of truth was meaning indeed for my good.

A Different World (1987–1993)

Season 4

Episode 23 If I Should Die Before I Wake (11 Apr. 1991)

gs: Whoopi Goldberg [Dr. Jordan], Tisha Campbell [Josie Webb]

"When you get up on this podium, I want you to look out in that audience and I want you to think to yourself, '**I'm a voice in this world damn it, and I deserve to be heard.**'"

TABLE OF CONTENTS

CHAPTER 1

MIRANDA RIGHTS

"You have the right to remain silent. Anything you say can and will be used against you in a court of law. You have the right to an attorney. If you cannot afford an attorney, one will be provided for you. Do you understand the rights I have just read to you? With these rights in mind, do you wish to speak to me?"

Being in a relationship with a narcissist is like being arrested and detained by the police, sent to trial before a judge, and sentenced to silence—regardless of what you did or did not do. They treat you like the Miranda rights say: *You have the right to remain silent.* But they will provoke you to speak, twist your words, and accuse you of the very things they do themselves. They will gaslight you to the point where you begin to gaslight yourself. You may even start to question your own sanity for putting up with such behavior.

Anything you say can and will be held against you. Anything you don't say can and will be held against you. They will get you to agree to unconventional things and attempt to sentence you to long-term silence. They silence you because it allows them to hide behind the faults they project onto you. They silence you because your voice is a threat—one that could expose them.

They treat you one way in private but show the world something entirely different in public. No one believes you at first when you speak up about what's bothering you. You may go quiet, caught in moments of cognitive dissonance. You can't believe that someone you once loved could treat you that way—then steal your voice, refuse to let you speak, talk over you, cloud your judgment, and make a fool of you. They tell you that you're crazy, that it's all in your head, that you're making things up.

Remember - they did that to your love, your friendship, and your devotion. They do not care. And now, as you try to explain it, it feels like no one hears you.

Furthermore, when it comes to Miranda rights and narcissists, you may need legal advice on how to deal with their behavior. You may even need a community of healers to help you navigate the stages of grief. The narcissist has likely faulted something about you every single day. They are committed to making you take the blame for everything that goes wrong. They are committed to shifting blame, avoiding accountability, and maintaining control over you.

If you ever resist their manipulation or advances—watch out. They'll change on you in an instant. The aim of this book is to help you find your voice in the room. Your voice matters. Now is the time to reclaim the power that is within you.

I'd rather my silence be misunderstood than my words be misquoted, or my presence mishandled.

~Morgan Richard Olivier

CHAPTER 2

PROLOGUE

You have been in a relationship that left you with more questions than answers. You find yourself googling behaviors just to understand someone you once believed was a good person. When you tell others, does it seem like no one understands what you're going through? Does it feel like no one hears you when you speak? Do you wonder if you're overthinking or just plain crazy?

You are not crazy. You may, however, be recovering from Complex Post-Traumatic Stress Disorder (C-PTSD) after dealing with a toxic individual or someone with narcissistic personality disorder (NPD).

When you were in a relationship with this person, did you often get interrupted when trying to express your point? Did they frequently avoid accountability by pointing out what *you* did instead? Did they beg you to share something important—only to later weaponize that information against you—hurting you so badly that you eventually just stopped talking? Conversations with them felt more like battles they were determined to win, rather than opportunities to understand you. Even when you tried to speak up, you found yourself holding your peace for so long it felt like you lost your voice.

You tried being direct.

You tried sugarcoating.

You tried inviting a neutral party—only to watch them twist the narrative, becoming the victim or the hero while painting you as the villain.

When you attempt to share your experience with a narcissist, it often sounds so unbelievable that even saying it aloud gives you a visceral reaction. Whether the narcissist is your father, mother, sibling, child, friend, spouse, spiritual leader, or supervisor, the common thread is this: they are selfish, self-centered, lack empathy, and they are capable of robbing you of the very essence of who you are.

But here's what you must remember:

You are strong.

You are a warrior.

You are more than a conqueror.

You *survived* their abuse.

This book will revive, inspire, and encourage you. It will make you aware of the tactics that were used to tear you down. Most importantly, it will remind you that you are not alone. Others have walked this path—and there are communities of survivors and healed individuals ready to help you navigate your recovery.

The narcissist tried to break you, but the words of this book are here to build you back up.

Its purpose is to help you rediscover your voice after years of being silenced by the cunning tactics of those with narcissistic traits or personality disorders.

The deep critical thinker has become the misfit of the world; this is not a coincidence. To maintain order and control you must isolate the intellectual, the sage, the philosopher, the savant before their ideas awaken people.

-Carl Jung

When you were triggered out of your mind as a kid, and no one helped you, and then you got blamed for it, parts of you decided you were a freak, burden and that you deserved it.

- Unknown

CHAPTER 3

YOUR VOICE

Do you realize that your voice can be used for so many things? From the moment you wake up until you go back to sleep, your voice can be in constant use. It can be used for communication, storytelling, teaching, poetry and spoken art, singing, acting, debate, protest, advocacy, voice voting, public speaking, social and emotional connection, expressing emotions, starting and ending wars, offering comfort and reassurance, making announcements, broadcasting—and the list goes on.

I want to emphasize the importance of using your voice. Speaking up and asserting yourself is crucial to maintaining your dignity and self-respect. When dealing with narcissistic behavior, it's essential to stay grounded and not lose sight of your truth. Your voice is a powerful tool that can break through manipulative tactics and bring clarity to situations which may otherwise be clouded by deceit. Remember - your perspective and experiences are valid, and no one has the right to undermine them. Stand firm in your convictions, and don't allow anyone to silence you. Your voice is a beacon of strength and resilience, illuminating the path to your empowerment.

Your voice holds immense value in countless ways. It is the means through which you communicate your thoughts, emotions, and beliefs, allowing you to connect with others and share your unique perspective. Speaking up not only asserts your presence but also affirms your identity, proving that you deserve respect and consideration. Moreover, your voice has the potential to influence and inspire those around you. It can challenge misconceptions, drive change, and foster understanding. By expressing your ideas and standing up for your principles, you contribute to the collective dialogue and help create a more inclusive and empathetic world.

In times of adversity your voice can be a source of courage, providing the strength needed to face challenges and advocate for what is right. It can break down barriers and dismantle oppressive narratives, empowering both yourself and others who may be experiencing similar struggles.

Ultimately, your voice is a testament to your resilience and tenacity. It reflects your spirit and your unwavering determination to uphold your truth. Embrace the power of your voice—let it guide you through life's complexities and illuminate the path to personal growth and societal progress.

Lastly, don't be discouraged by initial setbacks or resistance when using your voice. Persevere, and continue to practice and refine your communication skills. The more you assert your voice, the more comfortable and confident you will become in any setting. Use it.

The only way to find your voice is to use it. It's hardwired, built into you. Talk about the things you love. Your voice will follow.

Austin Kleon

Realize that some people aren't loyal to you, they are loyal to the need of you. Once their need changes, so does their loyalty.
                            ~Anavell Endayao

CHAPTER 4

WHAT IS A NARCISSIST?

What is a Narcissist?

Narcissist seems to be the latest buzz word for people others have a challenging relationship with. Before labeling everyone with boundaries, morals, and standards which you do not agree with as a narcissist, understand that not everyone will not let you walk all over them, talk to them any kind of way, and make them your doormat and yes man/woman. Some people have boundaries, standards, morals, character, integrity, and are protective of that respectfully. The official diagnostic definition of narcissistic personality disorder describes an individual with impairments related to identity, self-direction, empathy, and intimacy. A narcissist is someone who has an inflated sense of their importance, a deep, insatiable need for admiration, and a lack of empathy for others.

Narcissists are individuals with diametrically opposed views or opinions that go against their actions. They are meretricious. Narcissists are expert manipulators and often have multiple personalities. One personality is the persona, also known as the "mask," which they put on for the world to see, which is usually to give the perception of perfection.

Narcissists are fickle-minded creatures that love shiny new objects. They love to replace them (it) just as swiftly as they obtained them (it). The objects can be a variety of things known as supply. Supply can be superficial things used to keep the illusion of normalcy going. This may include houses, fancy cars, money, people, name brands, jobs, or anecdotal stories about things they have accomplished.

According to Jackson Mackenzie in an article at Psychopath Free,

"You have encountered pure evil. Everything you once understood about people did not apply to this person. During the relationship, you tried to be compassionate, easygoing, and forgiving. You never could have known that the person you loved was actively using things against you. It just does not make any sense. And so, you spent your time projecting a normal human conscience onto them, trying to explain away their inexplicable behavior. But once you discover psychopathy, sociopathy, or narcissism, everything starts to change. You begin to feel disgusted—horrified that you let this darkness into your life. Everything clicks and falls into place. All of the 'accidental' or 'insensitive' behavior finally makes sense. You try to explain this to friends and family members, but no one really seems to get it. This is why validation matters. When you come together with others who have experienced the same things as you, you discover you are not crazy. You are not alone in this human experience.[1]"

"Narcissism is a shame disorder, and narcissistic supply is what a narcissist gets from other people to mirror, validate their mask, and avoid the deep-rooted shame underneath their grandiosity."[2] A narcissist is a spectacularly and unbelievably selfish human being. They are world-class selfish. They will try to be all you could ever want and, in the end, not meet your needs. Narcissists are energy vampires. They are parasites in human form. They are never wrong. They are only nice to you to get what they want. After being with you a while, they are incredibly critical of you. But they are hypersensitive about any criticism of any kind. You, to them, are never good enough. Never were and never will be. EVER.

It is estimated that [the United States of] America has a population of 340 million people as of the 2025 U.S. Census Bureau. It is also noted that an estimated 1% to 2% of the population is narcissistic. This means that there are some 3.4 to 6.8 million narcissistic personalities in the United States of America alone. [3] Around 1% of adults in the general

1   Jackson Mackenzie. *Psychopath Free: Recovering from Emotionally Abusive Relationships with Narcissists, Sociopaths, and Other Toxic People.* Burkley, New York, New York. 2015.

2   LaKeisha Fleming. Medically Review by Ivy Kwong, LMFT. *Narcissistic Supply Explained: An insight into the mind of a Narcissist.* https://www.verywellmind.com/narcissistic-supply December 30, 2023.

3   http://www.cpsnews.com taken 1/23/2024.

community experience NPD, although some studies estimate this figure to be up to 6%. The data on NPD is unclear about whether this diagnosis is more common in men or women. Narcissists are not always 100% narcissistic; you might have someone who only has narcissism when certain events trigger it, e.g., when they are rejected or go through a hard time, and as a result, their personality disorder comes to the fore. On the other hand, you might deal with someone who is narcissistic all of the time, but not to a huge degree. These are the types of people you may be able to help, but anyone who is 100% severe and toxic in terms of narcissism, do not even bother trying to help. These people will not take your suggestions well, and they only way that these types of narcissists will ever help is when they take everything a step too far.[4]

Once you figure out that you are dealing with a narcissist, you figure their game out and you are not able to be manipulated by their games, they become droll, insipid, and very predictable. Nothing humbles the narcissist. Not getting caught in lies. Not getting exposed. Neither does the threat of danger or threat of jail time. Furthermore, losing you is no threat either since they have back-up supply, and losing you plays into their delusional game of being victim in their own narrative story. The steps of narcissistic abuse are

---

4   Murphy, Victor. *Highly Sensitive Empaths and Narcissists: The Empath's survival guide to healing from Toxic Relationship. Discover your skills, Understanding your gift, and stop being a victim of Narcissistic Abuse.* USA. 2019.

1. Love bombing/Idealization, 2. Devaluation, 3. Discarding / Reverse Discarding, 4. Hoovering, and 5. Repetition. They may vacillate between these in different variations, but the technique is the same. Narcissists are not to be trusted.

They view others [spouse, children, family members, friends, church, employees] as extensions of themselves. They also view most people through suspicious eyes as they are cynical. Because of their cynicism they attempt to remain vigilant about any word or deed which might challenge their perceived superiority or lack thereof. Narcissists live in a constant state of duality. With them, nothing is ever good enough.

They are never fully satisfied. You will find yourself going crazy trying to make them happy. The very things they love about you in the beginning of the relationship are the very things they will hate/envy you for later in the relationship. Why? Because they are gentle reminders of how miserable and empty their lives are. A narcissist may have pathological envy towards you. They may become green with envy when you are successful even with apparent failures that you learned from and shortcomings that still worked out.

The narcissist probably tried to undermine your success or sabotage you and it did not work. Shahida Aribi, MA gives a few examples found in an article written PsychCentral's .

1. The inability to congratulate others on a job will done.

2. A constant redirection to oneself when he/she is not the center of attention.

3. Contempt and condescension

4. Minimization and misattribution

5. Perpetually moving the goal posts of enough-ness[5]

In a narcissist's mind, they are never wrong and you are never right. Never. Which means you are always wrong, and they are always right. They will argue with you to prove this point. You will be in a discussion, and they will create a heated fellowship and disagree or change the answer just to prove something. Why? Because they are in competition with you, unbeknownst to you. They are trying to win, but you are trying to impart knowledge and get understanding. None of that matters to them. Winning against you in any way makes them feel accomplished.

Four key elements of narcissism are:

◊ Grandiosity

◊ Extreme self-focus

◊ An inflated sense of self-importance(s)

◊ A strong need for praise and recognition

A person with NPD will often have all of these signs to a great extent, all the time. Those with tendencies, but not the disorder, may display one or two, but to a lesser degree and only at certain times.[3]

Narcissists mirror you, then devalue you, and because they mirror you so much, they mirror the devalued you too

5   Shahida Aribia, *MA. 5 Ways Pathologically Envious Narcissists Undermine Your Success.* August 14, 2017 https://psychcentral.com/blog/recovering-narcissist/2017/08/5-ways-pathologically-envious-narcissists-undermine-your-success#1

and get upset because you are no longer strong, bright, or shiny like a new toy. They may be the bane of your existence all while telling you it is your fault that things are the way they are. In case you did not know this, the narcissist is simply trying to clone you. But when they devalue you and no longer see you as ideal, it creates a love/hate thing within them. Thus, they take it out on the nearest person - you.

Narcissists are essentially horrible, scary, evil monsters. Narcissists appear powerful, but in reality they are afraid of many things. Narcissists perceive attacks everywhere when there are no attacks.

This mental block for them causes them to think that you are always attacking them in several ways. You may notice how they have to exert strong control over you. This is a clear sign of how much they fear you. They are afraid of you having your own thoughts, feelings, and opinions. They accuse you of things you are not doing because of their fear that you are trying to persecute and humiliate them.

The narcissist lacks empathy. For them, life is always about securing supply at all costs. What is supply? Supply is a term used to describe who or what is used by the narcissist to meet some type of physical, money, or emotional need. They are pleasure-driven and not logic-driven.

They may be getting money, external validation, sex, attention, negative supply, ego strokes, and other things that help them continue to project their "false sense of self" to others. In the coming chapters, this will be explained in more detail. It is important to recognize that not all people with

NPD will look, act, or behave the same way. For example, one person with NPD could be a well-dressed, charming overachiever who cultivates a certain image to impress others.

Another person with NPD could be an underachiever who sets low expectations for themselves because of a sense of entitlement. Some researchers refer to narcissistic traits like a sense of authority, and a drive to become self-sufficient as **adaptive narcissism**.[6]

These traits can actually help a person succeed in certain areas of life, such as their career, education, or finances.[7] On the other hand, narcissistic traits like being exploitative, condescending, and aggressive are called maladaptive narcissism because they negatively affect the person who shows them and the people that they interact with.

Narcissists do not care who they hurt in the process of acquiring supply. This includes their spouse, children, friends, coworkers, associates, business partners - and the list goes on and on. In many instances they do not care what they must do to secure the supply. They will lose their inhibitions to secure supply. Thus, their entire adult life is transactional. They may use their own body in exchange for supply.

They may use the truth or false information for supply. They may use your negative reactions to their behavior as a supply. They may even use their children for supply. For narcissists, every person they meet is a potential new supply. All their developed relationships are stunted because all

---

6   https://www.verywellhealth.com/narcissistic-personality-disorder
7   Ibid

they can think about is getting something in exchange for something. Thinking, how can this person benefit me? What can I use them for? Quid Pro Quo, if you will.

They are stuck thinking, "What about me?" "What do I get for doing this?" "What is in it for me?" "How can I get them to do it all and I get the credit?" "I have to use what I've got to get what I want." "How can I hook this new supply for the long haul?"

In addition, narcissists cannot stay in places for prolonged periods of time. They love to move from one city, job, or person to another to avoid detection.

They may mask this by getting promotions in jobs which require them to relocate biannually. This provides the perfect cover for the shift-shaping narcissist to escape detection. They may be the new kid on the block, the new girl next door, or the person who just relocated to get a fresh start.

Narcissists get bored easily. So, the constant need for new supply and new locations is all the craze for them. It should be noted that narcissistic behavior is rooted in insecurity; namely an unfulfilled need to feel special or important. Children often received this feeling growing up - but not the narcissist.

This means that a narcissist has challenges experiencing genuine feelings of love. To compensate, they may replicate what they deem as appropriate expressions of love by mimicking romantic gestures or words without fully understanding the feeling behind them. Narcissistic abuse follows a particular formulaic pattern: love bombing, devaluating, discarding, hoovering and repeating. The abuse cycles are so predictable when you catch onto the pattern. The quickest way to break free is by understanding the script.

All relationships that narcissists are in are exclusively for their own gratification. Often, no one knows the damage the narcissist is inflicting on their victims. It is invisible, but over time it becomes obvious if you study the reactions of the victims. The cheating narcissists view their cheating as merely getting their needs met, but if you cheat, they will always remind you of your infidelity as this gives them an edge to guilt trip, shame, and insult you with.

Narcissists are sneaky. They cheat for the sport of it. They lack care for others, so cheating is purely for ego strokes and securing supply as they are not mature enough to establish meaningful relationships. If it is any consolation, they are not happy with you or the person with whom they are cheating.

They do not trust either of you. The children of narcissists are merely an extension of the narcissist. Their jobs, their marriages, their children, and their achievements are all extensions of the narcissist's ego.

The whole relationship with a narcissist is a fake. The whole thing is a façade, a counterfeit, a doppelganger, a hoax, a camouflage suit. It is make-believe, a fairytale, an imposter pretending to be sagacious but it is a buffoon and imbecile. They are professional thespians who out act the greatest actors Hollywood has ever seen and awarded. It is a masquerade ball with many masked marauders. It is Halloween masks and costumes everyday with them. When they can no longer control you, they attempt a smear campaign. The smear campaign is birthed within the narcissist from their need to be right and have their "truth" become the dominant script and retain their status to hide the shame of public exposure as a fake.

By controlling or rewriting the narrative of why they do what they do, they believe they maintain control of their image. The male or female narcissist curates this public persona very carefully; reflecting the appearance of success, accomplishments and being important.

The narcissist's show of care is an act. This type of narcissist is the altruistic narcissist. That altruistic narcissist is very generous and benevolent with what they have. However, they are pretending to show concern.

It is not genuine. Be assured they only care how your pain, lack, or trouble will affect their access to supply. If you stop being the main supply in any way, and they will cheat, get the money from somewhere else, threaten to leave, guilt trip, harass, manipulate you to work harder all while you come to notice that they do not help.

They only future-fake in order to get you enough dopamine to get back up and try harder. They wear the mask and one day that mask is going to slip, and when you discover that they were a lying, manipulating, empty soul of a human being, they are going to change from nice to nasty quick. You were tricked, hoodwinked, bamboozled.

They pulled a Kansas City shuffle and pulled smoke and mirrors. That is what happened to you. They studied you. They mirrored you. They pretended to hate stuff about you, but cloned the very behavior, phrases, and likeness of you when you adjusted your behavior to make it seem like they were the one. Then they reflected you back to you to lure you in and get you hooked.

The narcissist may have had a child with you, purchased a house with you, opened a business with you, or done something that will hook you to them for years, thus keeping you in a long-term cycle of supply to and for them and their games. They are smart enough to trap you and keep you locked in as they simultaneously seek and groom the next supply.

Narcissists will likely never change. Even if they become self-aware narcissists, it does not mean they change who they are. Their character and integrity are set. They have only become aware of their behavior, which in turn could make them more of a narcissist. The only hope for change is intense psychotherapy, but even with that, they may lie to the therapist and become a better, more cunning narcissist.

The biggest mistake you can ever make is thinking they will ever change for you. The only thing that will change about them is the shift shape they make. They may realize that they could lose you as the main supply. So, they adjust and then circumstances allow them to slide back into the lazy, goldbricking phase. A narcissist is going to be to you all you ever dreamed of, until they hook you. Then they change. They may start breadcrumbing you with morsels of the wonderful experience from the past. Then flip and discard you for someone else. You will experience the arrogance and the unmitigated gall and the audacity they display. Next, the entitlement of these individuals have is so great that they do not even consider the consequences of their actions.

The narcissist is bothered the most by having ask for help or to do things for others. It pains them because of their mentality of entitlement. However, they expect you to do almost everything for them. In the beginning they gave the appearance of being supportive, working with you in harmony and unity.

After a while, they let you do more until they stopped doing things altogether. No matter how much you do, it is never enough for them. The more you can do, the better for them. In front of others, they act benevolent and caring, but after they give, expect a guilt trip and smart remarks about you taking from them.

Narcissists will use anything you have disclosed to them against you. Your secrets, deepest fears, past traumas, and personal health information are all open games for the narcissist to use against you. Then, they will use your reactions to their chronic abuse as "evidence" that you are unstable and lack credibility, especially if you try to hold them accountable in the future. Narcissists may poke the bear until the bear reacts. Then, they record the reaction as evidence that it is not them who is the one that acts unconventionally. This is called reactive abuse.

A new year may dawn, and they may say, "New year, new me." That is a lie. Unless they are going to intense psychotherapy, are self-aware, and are doing shadow work to improve themselves, they will not change. They will just shift shape and camouflage the real them. Narcissists are extremely selfish people. They do not care about the hurt they cause unless it will end their supply or cause them shame.

When people show you who they are, believe them the first time.

~Maya Angelou

CHAPTER 5

MALE AND FEMALE NARCISSISTS' BEHAVIOR

This chapter is about male and female narcissists. I refer to them in this chapter as male and female narcissists because they are not mature enough to be considered adults. Furthermore, if you see the term men and women used here, it is because the source referenced stated it that way.

Narcissists are temper-tantrum toddlers, with teenage mentalities. So, it is difficult to refer to them as adults when they are children trapped in adult bodies. At best, they are adult-age males and adult-age females with the mentality of teenagers. However, they perceive themselves as gods, and desire worship and adoration and complete allegiance from their suppliers.

7.7% of men will develop NPD in their lifetime, versus only 4.8% of women, meaning that narcissism is much more common in men than in women.[8] The specific narcissistic tendencies someone exhibits depends on varied factors, including their gender and the type of narcissism they have.

Both male and female narcissists lack empathy or compassion. Nothing negative or amoral they do to you bothers them at all. In their mind, you deserved it, or they were entitled to do something to make them feel good. Both parties are capable of cheating and blaming you for it. Both are capable of lying and manipulating. Both fake love and relationships. They may have different ulterior motives but they both are super selfish.

They both are super self-centered. They lack empathy to the degree that when you tell them of an unpleasant experience, privately they will put you down for showing any emotions. Publicly they may show false empathy and then make snarling comments privately. This method is called a zinger. This is an insult in the middle of their statements. Much like dog whistling, the empath is the only one who knows and feels it coming. The narcissist only cares for their victim as supply. Their concern is only to keep the gravy train of supply going.

If there is a perceived threat to the supply, they will demonstrate what appears to be concern. You may mention that you are going to lose your job - they only care about the

8   Russ, E., et. al. (2008). Refining the construct of narcissistic personality disorder: Diagnostic criteria and subtypes. *American Journal of Psychiatry*, 165(11),1473-1481.

disruption of the supply. If you lose the ability to use your limbs, the narcissist will likely complain about having to take care of you. Again, they are only concerned with you being adequate supply. The narcissist having to take care of you and getting nothing in return is a big turn-off for them.

They may be a caregiver only in the aspect of a buzzard circling in the sky, waiting on a wounded animal to die so it can devour it. You could be going through a divorce, suffering identity theft, experiencing garnishment of wages, or be issued child support papers. Their true concern is how these issues will affect you being their steady supply.

Do not be fooled. All the fake love, fake care, and fake concern is to keep you as good supply. Once they find new suitable or replaceable supply that they deem can replace you, they will discard you and monkey branch over to the next person.

Some research suggests that covert narcissism and communal narcissism are more common in females, while overt and grandiose narcissism are more common in males. This difference may be at least partially explained by the different traditional gender roles created in society for adults, which is also believed to explain some of other key dissimilarities.

Another major difference is that narcissistic women tend to be focused on their physical appearance (sometimes called "somatic narcissism"), while their male counterparts are more likely to be driven by the desire for power and achievement.[9]

---

9   https://toxicties.com/narcissistic-behavior-men/ 4/3/2024

Coupled with a misogynistic belief that men are better leaders than women, and a pressure to be successful and dominant, these cultural messages are bound to create generations of narcissistic men.[10]

Manipulative tendencies, passive aggression, hypersensitivity to criticism, and shallowness or vanity are all more common signs of NPD in women. The female as well as male narcissists often manipulates the federal funding systems, child support systems, grants, loans, and other means to fulfil needs they does not want to do anything about.

The female may need assistance, but she may also seek to goldbrick and parasite off others' means as she gives the appearance of being a victim. Female narcissists may have multiple children from multiple well-to-do men and have each of them acting as supply for child support. This is a perfect victim story. Perfect place to hide. Perfect scenario to get an unsuspecting hero to come in and rescue her. Female narcissists are likely to use their beauty and sex to manipulate and get their way.

Remove sex from a relationship, you will discover that 90% of women have nothing to offer men in relationships. Conversely, remove money from a relationship, and you will learn that 90% of women will not see a reason to be in said relationship.

~ Richard Cooper

Both male and female narcissists can be materialistic. The male may enjoy focusing on making money. The female

---

10   Ibid.

may enjoy spending her supply's money. As a narcissist, he can never make or have enough. She, as a narcissist, can never spend enough. She may likely enjoy treating herself with the best and most expensive designer clothing. She likely revels in luxuries that someone else afforded her.

She is also spoiled by wealthy, well-to-do sugar daddies she has little-to-no feeling for. Both have to move very fast in the beginning of the relationship. Be assured that within a ninety-day window, they are in love, want to move in together, want to get married, can see themselves growing old with you, can see themselves having children with you, going into business with you and so on.

You to their fast moving, are the answer to the question. Love at first sight can happen, but the narcissist does not even know how to spell your name, met your family, or let you know who they are but are moving fast to hook you. Even most jobs do not offer full benefits until you have worked with them ninety days. But that narcissist thinks it should be instant benefits package for them much like the instant grits, rice and oatmeal.

Female narcissists are never wrong and can never be wrong. They can seldom, if ever, be corrected or criticized without causing narcissistic injury. She is overly sensitive to any perceived slight. She can dish out criticism but cannot receive it without feeling slighted. They always display themselves as the victim to everyone who listens to their side of the story. If the female narcissist thinks that someone doubts her lies or delusions of grandeur by speaking negatively of her, she will react quickly and fight back. She may go into a narcissistic collapse as people see through her façade, or she will become persnickety and turn molehills into mountains.

The male narcissist is professionally bored with certain aspects of life and goes through most of them like they're chores he did not sign up for when he has to be responsible and accountable for life not working like he imagines it to be. He vacillates between women and jobs, and lives with halfhearted, hairbrained ambitions.

The male narcissist believes that his existence as a male in the world grants him access to unlimited supply and that anyone who attempts to disprove this is a threat. He believes that the world has wronged him and dealt him a bad hand of cards to play with. Because he is used to getting his way, he sees no real reason to change, alter behavior, grow, and mature as a man. In other words, he is perfect, and you should accept him as he is - "Mr. Perfect." He will switch up with his next option if it appears it will yield more immediate gratification and results.

Delayed gratification is a no-no for both male and female narcissists. The male narcissist hates to work hard and for a long time, especially when apparent shortcuts to success are readily available. He may abandon his family, job, career, team, organization and anything else for self-aggrandizement. Today, he speaks of himself as if he were some type of god. When his god-like self-perception is not recognized by others, he goes into his cave of dark corridors of his mind. Drunk with images of himself being something he is not, when faced with failure he drinks the cups of pity from others but looks at them with disdain for ever thinking he needed the pity.

The male narcissist has no moral compass to guide his morality. His amygdala is stuck in fight or flight mode, pumping huge amounts of cortisol in his veins. He is never fully committed to anyone or anything. He moves from one temporary situation to another. This includes jobs, women, children, wives, parents, associates, and friends. He may shack up, become a professional gambler, drift from state to state, or become a career student, but he cannot fully commit to anyone or anything.

All his relationships with everything and everyone are shallow and are marked with envy and jealousy of others. When attempting to communicate, he may sulk and practice some form of passive-aggressive avoidance. The male has this subtle glare of envy when others are praised. In his mind, he should get the award. He should have been praised. He should be celebrated. But does a fish get an award for swimming? Does the bird get an award for flying?

However, the male and female narcissists feel they should get praise even when putting minimal effort into things. Every time someone else gets praise and compliments, it is a perceived threat to him, and he will get his revenge or act in some manner to show his disapproval.

Holidays with him are impossible because he will shift the focus and attention from group to individual. Both male and female narcissist will ruin any event that you are excited about. Birthdays, parties, graduations, vacations. If you are looking forward to it, they are looking forward to ruining it. Before you all go out, they will start a fight, have a breakdown, have an emergency they create. Understand this is deliberate.

They are classically conditioning you to not look forward to special events where they are not the highlight of. Much like a dog can associate a bell with food, every time the dog hears the bell it knows food is coming, that narcissist has something that is so important going one every time you or someone else is being celebrated. They have to be the center of attention at someone else's event.

The idea is the bring fear, anxiety stress in association with celebrations thus, you are not interested and associate major events with something that will go wrong. Bump that. I just exposed that game. Again, if it's a male, he is world-class selfish.

He's much like the child that has the only ball in the neighborhood but, when others pick the team and he is picked last or does not get to establish the rules, he will take his ball; the male narcissist will withdraw his time, resources, agreement, contractual agreements, energy, and participation if he perceives he will not be given a thunderous applause for his contributions.

The female narcissist has an insatiable appetite for attention and external validation from others. This may cause her to become vain and have an overly heightened sense of her appearance. She may keep superficial things going to keep her appearance up such as fake hair, fake nails, fake eyes, fake breasts, injections, a pseudonym to give when she meets others out of town, excessive makeup to cover her aging, and lots of cosmetic surgery. The female narcissist only has beauty and intimacy to offer, not real substance. Thus, she can attempt to keep her form, figure, and attention as she is unable to reverse the aging process.

Her false self is well disguised amid these externally validating items. She fixes the outside but never the inside, because she is never wrong in what she is doing. Research has found an association between certain facets of narcissism and malicious envy. It is no surprise, then, that the female narcissist is driven by malicious envy in her treatment of other women she feels threatened by.

Female narcissists become visibly irate and can become extremely aggressive in response to another woman's attractiveness, success, popularity, or all of the above. Malicious envy is an active destructive form of envy where the female narcissist attempts to sabotage or belittle the envied target through acts of hostility, contempt, bullying, slander, exclusion, covert put-downs, smear campaigns, and other forms of relational aggression.

While women who "just" internalized misogyny may feel occasionally jealous or envious of others, narcissistic women are distinct in that they go out of their way to excessively bully, mock, and belittle those they are envious of.[11]

---

11   Shahidi Arabia, MA. 5 Attitudes including malicious envy expose malignant Narcissists, According to Research https://psychcentral.com/blog/recovering-narcissist

A real man understands that sex isn't everything when it
comes to satisfying a lady…Comforting her, appreciating her,
respecting her…and taking care of her emotionally is also part of
pleasing her.

~Bryan Burden

Male narcissists tend to become online trolls more often than the female narcissists. You may observe how misogynistic they are. They may be addicted to working out in the gym to sculpt and keep a perfect body to maintain stamina for escapades. The male narcissist deliberately and intentionally puts down and disrespects women, especially the women they are in relationships with and are married to. They may also do it to the women they work with. They may use fear and intimidation, coercion, exploitation, and a series of other behaviors in an attempt to control women.

Male narcissists tend to have an overinflated ego as well as an overinflated sense of their importance which is masked by objects to demonstrate their wealth. This may include treasures, art, fancy cars, a large house, and access to celebrities. They may even use their wealth to have inappropriate kinds of relationships that leave a trail of victims in the wake. Please know that they do not care about people as anything more than supply of some kind - supply for sex, validation, self-aggrandizement, status, influence, and power.

The male narcissist will surround themselves with people, affectionally known as flying monkeys, which tend to feed into their false self. The male narcissist may use his wealth to foster relationships that he would not be able to gain without his wealth. The male narcissist may have to have copious amounts of attention. The perfect hideaway is the internet, with social media and chatrooms as the main supply. On the internet you can be anyone you want. This is known as "catfishing."

The male often seeks lonely, trusting souls, plays manipulation games, and then dominates their victims. Male narcissists are more likely to find ways to extort and embezzle money from people's accounts, get them to buy into their delusion of grandeur dream that only needs a financial boost that the victim just happens to have, and ruin their credit, drain the bank accounts, empty the IRAs, 401ks, trust funds, CDs, and all other forms of financial security.

He must be in a dominant position at all times publicly as his false self is of the utmost importance to camouflage his fragile ego, while privately he may do things like cross-dressing, role play, deal with people less than half his age, and do other things to compensate for his lack of maturity.

Some female narcissists may claim they are on a healing journey and want to heal past traumas or generational curses. But, there is no evidence to support their claims of doing any of these things. There are no self-help books, no support groups, and no therapy on the horizon for her, but she complains and plays the victim. There is no quantifiable evidence to present with her claims except that she wants to. The female narcissist has excuse after excuse when it comes to them holding up their end of a bargain. They paint themselves as the poor, victimized, left-out wife, or the unappreciated girlfriend. They are the self-sacrificing one in the relationship. If the female narcissist decides to go to the therapist, like the male narcissist, she will probably attempt to manipulate the therapist. She believes because she is a female, and she gets married, she is entitled to special privileges and accommodations, and if you do not give these to her, she is well within her right to get them by any means necessary.

The male narcissist feels the same in the sense that he should get whatever he wants because he is entitled to it. The female narcissist wants the man to take care of her at one end of narcissism. She may desire to be treated as a queen bee in a beehive; special, and the only one that gets to do and get away with certain things. She gets in a relationship with a certain kind of man.

She will get pregnant right away and decide to be a stay-at-home spouse. On the other end of the spectrum is the working female narcissist who will lord it over her significant other that she works and makes just as much or more money than them. It is a power struggle for her to gain the authority of the relationship. What better way for either the male or female narcissist to do so than to try to control the finances?

Female narcissists are exhausting for manly men to be around. Her constant never-ending demands and her jabs at his masculinity are intolerable over time. She will counter every aspect of his leadership skills. She is almost always ungrateful and creating chaos where there is peace. Trying to keep her satisfied while constantly walking on eggshells to keep her from being set off will eventually drain the lifeforce out of a person as a never-ending chore.

In a recorded interview with Sadia Khan, Lewis Howes asks her why 70% of relationships end in the first year.

Lewis – "Why do we see so many women causing frustration in their relationship when they start dating a man based on a wound that someone else did and not the man in front of them?"

Sadia – "Because we have created a generation of narcissistic women. The rise of social media and the rise of online dating, and the rise of feminism, have taught women that they are not to blame for any poor choices. So, if you wanna be a sex worker, it is great. If you wanna post a bikini picture online, it is fine. Every poor choice is glamorized and there are terms for internal reflection seen as gaslighting yourself. So, they have got terms for internal reflection to prevent this happening.

So, what will happen is they are trained to not reflect on themselves because we have been told we've been oppressed for so many years, so now it's time to make sure we project. And so, we do not take any accountability, and as a result when we get into relationships if we don't feel completely soothed all the time he must be a narcissist. He must be a manipulator. He must be gaslighting. He. He. He. rather than I. I. I. And unfortunately, we have an online market that caters to that wounded woman, that caters to that entitled woman, that caters to that narcissistic woman. And it is so wild to me that women talk about narcissism, but the society caters to the narcissistic woman."

Sadia continues – "If I post a picture online a bikini picture online, there is nothing my husband could do that could compete with that level of attention and validation."

Lewis – "Yeah, the compliment, the consumer the messaging that you're so sexy and all these different things."

Sadia - There is nothing he can do. He cannot post online and get the same level of validation. So, what has happened is we've created a setup in society that means men have to compete with the level of validation, with which they can't compete.

And if women go online, if they join Tinder that night, they can have so many more options than a man can....but the things I can do to manipulate male validation and get more attention from that just soothe myself and remind myself, 'I'm above this.' 'I don't need him.' 'I can replace him.' We say something men actually can't do so they have to rely on pornography for that. We replaced him for likes and the men, they replace us with pornography.[12]"

Sadia concludes that persuasive ending result of these behaviors for men and women in relationships leads to intense and pervasive loneliness. She argues that until we wake up to the impact of technology, for men and women, it is going to lead to complete identity crisis, self-inflicted, low external intrinsic values, depression, and external validation.

---

12   Interview Sadia Khan and Lewis Howes Full video Http://youtu.be/ ExaMJRg5xks?si=jmAqDtYLuQEJVz23

Men will not commit because they can get all the joys of a sexual relation without having to commit. Women can get all the validation of male attention without having to adapt and commit to the needs of the relationship. Therefore, we have a society of males and females that do not need each other for relationships.

A female narcissist will guilt trip you and shame you for pointing out any things that she needs to address and work on as a functioning adult. By calling her out, you will cause narcissistic injury, and she is going to get her revenge on you.

That revenge could be gaslighting, discarding you, serial cheating, invalidating your opinions, being disagreeable with anything you say [no matter how miniscule it is], being highly critical of everything you do, breadcrumbing you, rationing out sex, withholding affection, attempting to turn children you have together against you, starting a smear campaign, trying to give you false hope, spending all your earned and invested money on frivolous things, or abandoning the relationship.

Either way, she is on a mission to pay you back, and she will not be satisfied until she feels it is enough repayment. How much is enough? It is never enough. You will be on an endless downward spiral for your causing them narcissistic injury.

Some common excessive behaviors in narcissistic females:

◊ A need for attention and admiration
◊ Feeling pleasure from the pain of others

◇ An extreme sense of entitlement
◇ Actively practicing and engaging in misandry
◇ A tendency to exploit others for their own benefit
◇ Manipulative and controlling behavior
◇ Dramatic emotional behavior
◇ Inability to accept constrictive criticism without having a narcissistic collapse
◇ Dramatic emotional behavior/rage
◇ Being persnickety and not seeing the bigger picture

As a contrast, the male narcissist will often team up with his mother or guardian to destroy the partner he is in a long-lasting relationship with. He comes from a toxic, codependent relationship. His mother probably despises him because his father did not validate her. The male child narcissists are a gentle reminder of the man that did not validate her. His mother then invalidates him. Thus, he hates his mother and becomes a male chauvinistic; an egomaniacal maniac.

When it comes to cheating, the female narcissist would rather tell you than for you to discover that she is cheating. When she cheats, it is often for the thrill of it, and the ones she cheats with are your replacement as she is only seeking validation and supply.

The shame associated with her being discovered and exposed is almost too much to bear, and she would likely rather end the entire relationship than admit to wrongdoing and take full accountability for her actions, because she is always right anyway. In her mind, she is entitled to compensate for her partner's lack. She will likely gaslight you with infidelity by saying it is your fault she cheated. But do not be fooled. Nothing is good enough for the narcissist. She is willing to lose you when she starts serial cheating. All cheating is a deliberate and intentional act. It is all planned and thought out thoroughly prior to the action by female narcissists. No matter what her mouth says, she thought about it, planned it, and acted on it all with selfish intention.

Male narcissist who cheat, want out of the relationship too. Male narcissists cheat for more varied reasons than female narcissists. Females are often driven by their emotions. Their emotions tie them to the one they cheat with emotionally and physically. However, male narcissists cheat for sport. Someone may have bet on them or dared them that they could not do it. The people the males cheat with is there to get them through their need for that time.

Remember, neither male nor female narcissists are capable of real love. They are only interested in what is in it for themselves. So, it is not real with the new supply either. Also, with the phone and internet available, both the male and female have constant access to old, new, and potential supply. Right now, your male or female narcissist probably has people in their phone under pseudonyms who are their old or new supply.

Right now, your male or female narcissist has internet trolls and inboxes, DMs, and other internet schemes going on that you know little to nothing about. Their phone is the key. They take that phone with them everywhere when they have an interesting supply. They have it in the bed. They move it out of reach when they wake up. They wake up in the middle of the night conversing and communicating with their supply. They take it to the bathroom and kitchen when they want a snack, and it's with them when they go to the mailbox or just to turn on the air. They are almost always with their phone. Their supply may communicate, and they may miss it, so they have to have it with them at all times.

Another key factor to consider is how male and female narcissists operate with communication. Some females communicate by talking and bouncing ideas off others. The female narcissist is communicating to be right. She is in a competition to win and if it seems like she is going to lose, she may revert to using word salads, playing emotional gymnastics, overtalking, interrupting you in mid-sentence, stonewalling, and passive aggressive tones.

You may be dealing with a gaslight goddess. She will literally convince you that your truth is invalid and her truth is what matters as reality. She wants to be heard and validated. She, like the male, thinks she knows more than you, and her conversing with you is from a stance of superiority to inferiority. Both male and female narcissists are likely not going to read any self-help books because they see themselves as know-it-alls. If you purchased a book for them to read to gain new information, they may feel insulted and reject all the advice the book offers. Please keep in mind that they already think they do no wrong and are perfect even in their flaws.

Moreover, when communicating, the female narcissist wants her expertise heard. If the female narcissist is with a man, she probably does not know what to do with his silence. There are times when men are silent, and nothing is wrong - such as simply not talking while riding in a car during a multi-hour drive. If a man is silent, it can leave the narcissistic female in a state of shock. She must know what you are thinking so she can counter it.

On the contrary, if the female narcissist is caught in a wrong, she will answer a question with a question as a method to deflect. In general, the more something is bothering a female, the more she will talk about it. The more you will keep hearing it. Silence is a weapon as she must now try to figure out what you are thinking. Male narcissists are on the other side of the spectrum with communication. The more things which bother males, the less you are likely to hear him talk about it.

There is almost a dead silence to men when things are really bothering them. He can literally not mention what is bothering him for years, and you would never get a whiff of it anywhere. He may use insulting jokes or make jabs at you. He may use subtle putdowns that no one else catches. He could be plotting to abandon his family and never give a sign in conversation ever. He can bring flowers, pay the bills, open the doors, even help around the house, and still be planning his exodus from you.

As it relates to verbiage, the male narcissist will use silence to punish his wife, girlfriend, or significant others. Male narcissists are likely to be arrogant and cocky and make cutting remarks that give you death by a thousand cuts. He may refer to somebody's weight, health, or other issues and cause private, unseen pain.

Some of the most common excessive behaviors in narcissistic males include:

◊ He is driven by his need to control
◊ He sees you as a possession, not a person
◊ Sexist ideas about women (misogyny)
◊ Monopolizes conversations
◊ Takes unnecessary risks
◊ Holds grudges forever
◊ Easily prone to anger that turns violent
◊ Bragging or exaggerating achievements

Not to worry though, that is what this book is for - to help you become a detective and identify the behaviors of these people so you can gain clarity and find your voice in the room.

The degree to which a person can grow is in direct proportion to the amount of truth they can accept about themselves without running away.
~Shannon Kaiser

CHAPTER 6

TYPES OF NARCISSISTS

1. **Covert** – These narcissists use methods which are behind the scenes. Usually only the victim knows the abuse they are suffering. They play the savior, while setting you up to have to do things for them in the future by guilt-tripping you with, "Remember when I..." Please understand - they are also charming, they display a counterfeit identity, they are liars, they're manipulative with an extreme sense of entitlement and they lack empathy. They also exploit others, and are destructive in relationships, They're con-artists who have an excessive need for admiration, along with a victim consciousness. Lastly, they lack remorse for the effect of their words and deeds.

2. **Overt** – These narcissists are more direct in the pursuing of their needs. They lack concern for being discovered because they know how to play their victims.

3. **Invulnerable** – Individuals with vulnerable narcissism tend to be insecure, self-victimizing (woe is me) and

sensitive to rejection. They may require constant validation from others, and be masters of self-victimization. They may experience feelings of inadequacy, anxiety, and bouts of depression due to their thirst and hunger for outside approval.

4. **Altruistic/Communal Narcissist** – These narcissists are self-righteous, moral, and benevolent. Altruistic narcissists give the impression of being kind people because of their 'good deeds,' although they are likely to have an ulterior motive. An altruistic narcissist is someone who meets some or all of these criteria but who also displays kind and generous actions, appearing to be altruistic. However, unlike true altruists, they only behave this way in order to be admired, revered, or to expect a favor in return.

5. **Grandiose** –This narcissist uses bullying and contempt to prove they are winners.

6. **Malignant (Toxic)** – These narcissists are antisocial. They feel everyone is out to get them. They have moments of paranoia and schizophrenia. Their behavior is infectious to others.

7. **Amorous/Sexual** – These narcissists use love bombing and their sexual prowess to control and manipulate a relationship. The use their sex appeal for coercion and extorsion. Often kissing is too intimate for narcissists, so if they ever say, "things happened but we did not kiss", this could be a moment of honesty. They may involve themselves in a parasitic sexual relationship with people

to gain supply or with people who can help them in some way. They will triangulate you and make you jealous.

8. **Inverted** – These narcissists are parasites who leech on to their supply and are energy vampires, constantly draining victims of almost all their energy and resources. They are known for being a day late, a dollar short, 'let me get it on consignment and pay you back'.

9. **Antagonistic** – These narcissists are hostile, manipulative, and explosive in temper. Trivial things trigger them. They are also known for bullying, verbal threats and intimidation.

10. **Adaptive** – This refers to narcissistic traits like a sense of authority and a drive to become self-sufficient. These traits can help a person succeed in certain areas of life, such as their career, education, or finances. The narcissist will give a gentle reminder of who helped them get where they are. i.e., if it was not for me....

11. **Aging Narcissist** – For narcissists, aging can be considered a bursting of the narcissistic bubble. One such reason is because they cannot get as much supply as they did when they were younger, while some have less control over others and have become almost totally dependent on others since they did not invest properly in their youthful days. They have now become more entitled, less accountable, and they've often lost their sense of purpose and are unempathetic. They are a burden [mostly to their children or family members] and not an asset but a liability. They are also desperate and will do desperate

things to keep the supply going. If the narcissist is a female, she probably used sex as her means of exchange, and as she has gotten older, the crowd has shifted their attention to younger women. She may offer an open marriage to keep her man. If the narcissist is a man, he probably has money, influence, and connections. But, his influence and perversions have probably caught up with him. For each, their waning age is a gentle reminder of angst.

Traits of Narcissism Include

◊ Being overly boastful, exaggerating one's own achievements

◊ Pretending to be superior to others

◊ Lack of empathy for others

◊ Looking down on others as inferior

◊ Monopolizing conversations

◊ Impatience, anger, unhappiness, depression, or mood swings when criticized.

◊ Easily disappointed when expected importance is not given

◊ Always craving for "the best" in everything

◊ Having a very fragile self-esteem

◊ Careless and or reckless-style behavior with no regard for how it will affect others

◊ Pathological liar

◊ Blames victims but repeats the same destructive behaviors in all relationships

◊ Manipulates all dedicated events/holidays for their benefit

◊ Stating they feel no-one understands them

Imitation is the sincerest form of flattery that mediocrity can pay to greatness.
~Oscar Wilde

CHAPTER 7

NARCISSISTIC SUPPLY

Narcissists often view their supply as external extensions of themselves. They are in constant search of suppliers. A narcissist's supply consists of attention, admiration, respect, money, adulation, positive and negative emotions, and even fear. Supply for the narcissist may be pathological or excessive. "Narcissistic supply is the 'drug' that the narcissist is addicted to in order to feed their false self (their mask), and avoid their true self and the shame that comes along with that," explains Avigail Lev, PsyD, founder and director of Bay Area CBT Center.[13] Narcissists are not looking for love. They do not know what love is. They are looking for a new supply. Grade A supply. There are five specific types they seek.

1. Money (gravy train) to fund their façade.
2. Sex for ego, validation, or to hook the new supply.

---

13   LaKeisha Fleming. Medically Review by Ivy Kwong, LMFT. Narcissistic Supply Explained: An Insight into the Mind of a Narcissist. https://www.verywellmind.com/narcissistic-supply December 30, 2023.

3. A new/temporary place to stay, to avoid detection.

4. Ego boost/flattery to polish their false self.

5. Control at all times [even if they appear cooperative].

They often get this supply from codependent empaths, other narcissists, flying monkeys, and their new victims. Supply to the narcissist brings validation to the false self they created. Examples of supply include but are not limited to:

Spouse and kids – this gives the narcissist the appearance of being normal, social, and admirable.

Romantic relationships on the side – extra adoration, a sense of desirability, and sexuality.

Business – accomplishment and financial successes.

Cellphones – The cellphone of the narcissist is the key to their craftiness and most dangerous tool utilized to keep them connected with potential supply. It can be used for business, espionage, cheating, recording, and to get validation. The cell phone is also used for selfies [to worship themselves and seek idolization from others], to triangulate and keep up with their supply and potential supply [the ex, the next and you simultaneously], and for social media and internet access which gives them a seemingly endless supply and several avenues to cheat, wear the mask, catfish, start wars, and create content for attention.

Luxury Brands – this gives the appearance that they have finances and culture. The narcissist probably has luxury brands but not enough money in the bank to purchase these brands. They may even buy knock-offs to give onlookers the appearance that they can afford things too.

Social media fans/friends – external validation with likes, also a place to seek new supply, keep up with ex-lovers and find new partners to cheat with. [Also mentioned with cell phones]

Religious Affiliation – this gives a sense of respect, community involvement, and the sense of a moral compass.

Home, cars – their home and car serve to suggest to the onlooker that they belong in a certain community and have achieved a certain social status in life.

Money – Money is said to be the root of all kinds of evil. For the narcissist, it is a tool used to validate their false self. They use money to gain extrinsic favor, eccentric pleasure, and rewards. Money provides security, power, freedom, self-esteem, and admiration for what the perception of wealth gives. Money gives the narcissist the freedom to do and be who they want with it, which they otherwise could not be without it.

Please understand that everything that glitters is not gold. Furthermore, understand that each new thing to the narcissist is only a new toy that will get dull and lose its shine, as the narcissist is an impulse thinker and is mostly relying on living in the moment to create a mask to hide behind the shame.

We can look at narcissists' supply as control; their supply is, typically, someone who will be available to them whenever needed, who will not point out their flaws, and who will not hold them accountable for their actions. Narcissists have a need to control so that individuals around them do not see their flaws. With narcissists, almost everything is well-thought-out and calculated. If we do not reach out to them or reject them, they are going to realize that we are standing up for ourselves. Thus, given their addiction to the feeling of power, narcissists will then feel threatened and will go into desperation mode. It is crucial for a narcissist to have a primary supply, and in this situation, they might even get worried they will lose us as their primary supply.[14]

As you can see, the narcissist's supply is not someone that the narcissist 'loves' or is 'happy with'. They have simply been enlisted by the narcissist to provide them with an unlimited amount of narcissistic supply, which we now know is an impossible ask. Armed with this understanding, the narcissist is likely to not file for divorce in the marriage because their spouse is a source of supply.

They will keep the spouse, an ex and the next if it means they have a constant and assured source of supply. The female narcissist in particular is looking for a **P.H.I.L.** – Protector, Helper/Hero, Integrity, and Love. The supply she needs must be a protector. Someone who will stand up for her, defend her, and make sure no one else dares to threaten her reputation. Also, he must be willing to be a helper or be her hero and save

14   Krisztina Petho-Robertson. M.Ed., LPC. How Does a Narcissist Handle Rejection and No Contact. https://upjourney.com/how-does-a-narcissist-handle-rejection-and-no-contact

the day. She will often be a damsel in distress. Short on rent, just a few days away from payday but the due date is now? She will get the victim to be motivated here, which brings up the next phase. For the next thing she is looking for someone with integrity; someone who will do what they say, keep their promises, and do the right thing, including save her from her unwise decision-making.

And lastly, someone who is loving. Someone to love her for how she projects to be. Someone to love her false self so she can hide behind the mask. The covert female narcissist will use this **P.H.I.L** technique to lure, bait, and hook someone for the long haul.

Let me explain an example here. The female covert narcissist will position herself to date men she can practice this technique on. The style is hypergamy. It will likely begin with some sort of complaint about someone and how they are being treated or neglected. The complaint is linked to a problem that needs to be solved. This is a call for action for you to **protect** them.

Next, she will elevate it. Her baby's daddy, estranged husband, boss, father, stepfather, mother, or someone has wronged her. This call to action caused you to want to be their hero and save the day. She may claim to be short on money for a payment of something and not have the money. After that, she'll play on your integrity. She may get you to make a promise and hold you to keeping it. She may use the phrase, "You said you were going to....," "You told me you would give me...... if I did......." "Remember when you told me you would…I know you are going to keep your promise." Here is a little guilt trip but it is subtle; it may go over your head. Then, with the mix of guilt trip and your integrity they then go for the gusto. "If you loved me, you would not let me go through this." "If you loved me, then I should not have to do this by myself. You are my man; you are supposed to help."

The role of the new supply is to feed the narcissist's addiction for attention. You see, the narcissist learnt a lot from you. I can guarantee that those lessons will not go to waste but be put to clever use with the new supply. They will use all of the data they collected from you, plus bundle it together with what they learn about the new supply and apply it all throughout their current manipulations.

The narcissist will give the new supply everything that you wanted. Why? Because if you liked it, then why wouldn't the next person want it? Remember, without authenticity, empathy and kindness at hand, the narcissist is merely relying on data to pull off a successful Love Bomb. Lastly, they came to you after leaving someone else. They will eventually leave you, going to someone else.

They cannot help themselves. They probably have a laundry list of potential suppliers. Their ex, their next and you all at the same time. Even if one supply is steadier than the other, their self-destructive, selfish, manipulative behavior will cause them to lose it all and give them a new victim sob story to tell the next potential supply. For the record, it is okay to be the bad guy or villain in the story. The narcissist is always the victim. They will lie to get an advance with the next supply. Just remember, "Lies take elevators, the truth takes the stairs." With that being said, they are habitual liars.

Some narcissists, as long as they are getting sufficient supply, will stay for a prolonged period of time; even years. Some feel comfortable with one primary source of supply. This is called Grade A supply. Tyler Perry, in his play *Why did I get Married?* may have inferred to this in a manner, calling it the 80/20 rule. In this way, one source of supply may have approximately eighty percent of all the things someone could both want and need.

However, when things get common in relationships and the emotional love wears off and the thrills lessen, people seek the missing twenty percent and abandon the eighty for the twenty. They may get one hundred percent of the twenty and realize that the twenty lacks so much. By then it is too late. The damage is done. The narcissist chased a fantasy. They may cheat on you repeatedly, but they will stay as long as you let them.

They may not abandon you physically, but they will abandon you emotionally and in every other way. You may be in a relationship, but it feels like you are alone and lonely. [15] "Narcissism is a shame disorder, and narcissistic supply is what a narcissist gets from other people to mirror, validate their mask, and avoid the deep-rooted shame underneath their grandiosity."[16]

---

15   Maria Consiglio – internet quote.
16   LaKeisha Fleming. Medically Review by Ivy Kwong, LMFT. Narcissistic Supply Explained: An Insight into the Mind of a Narcissist.

I owe myself a little apology for being with people in spaces I KNEW I wasn't respected, wanted, appreciated, loved, or valued, but instead, I stayed for the sake of our history. I owe myself an apology for putting people who NEVER appreciated me before myself.

~ WomanCEOgossip

CHAPTER 8

TYPES OF NARCISSISTIC SUPPLY

Because their sense of self is determined by what others think of them, narcissists use relationships for self-enhancement. Everyone must feed them. In addition, they seek validation and attention in their public, private, and professional lives. Other people are used as objects in order to provide their supply. For example, they may need constant compliments or applause, more status and money, or they may check their appearance in the mirror several times a day. Some examples of narcissistic supply are:

1. Praise and compliments!
2. Accomplishments and professional success (even if by cheating or using unethical means)
3. Financial gain by any means
4. Status symbols such as a marriage, a big home, gold toilet, expensive car, works of art, 5-star dining and luxury hotels

5. Acquaintances with celebrities, public figures, and other high-status people and institutions

6. Wearing designer labels and expensive accessories and jewelry

7. Winning at everything at all costs, no matter what

8. Using <u>alcohol</u>, drugs, or other addictive substances

9. Sex [of all types (good and not good)]

10. Provoking arguments, emotional reactions, and chaos

11. Receiving awards

12. Attention in the news or <u>social media</u>

13. Being admired and loved by romantic partners

14. Having a mate that is desired by others, such as a trophy wife or influential or successful spouse.

15. Expressions of <u>gratitude</u>

Some people will only "love you" as much as they can use you.
Their loyalty ends where the benefits stop.
~ Unknown

CHAPTER 9

HOW DOES A NARCISSIST GET THEIR SUPPLY?

Other people are used as objects in order to provide their supplies. S. Freud identified two main paths to fulfilling narcissistic supplies: aggression and ingratiation. Eventually, he called them sadistic and submissive. To be admired and to get their supply, narcissists employ various strategies, including impression management. They ingratiate themselves using their charm, emotional intelligence, bragging, seduction, and manipulation. Receiving attention and admiration boosts their weak self and lack of self-esteem.

They manipulate and try to control what others think in order to feel better about themselves, making narcissists dependent on recognition from others. The narcissists will attempt to micromanage every aspect of your life. Losing control for them can cause a complete meltdown. If you refuse to provide what they want and need, they resort to their secondary means: aggression with narcissistic abuse. They go on the offensive, attack, and belittle you. By discounting you, in their eyes their self-image is elevated. This behavior is known as a smear campaign. In relationships, they can become sadistic. As their abuse escalates, their partners and coworkers become passive and submissive to avoid coming under attack and to maintain the relationship. By assuming a submissive role, they establish an unhealthy dynamic in relationships with a narcissist.

When the grandiose narcissist realized that the spell that was being cast worked but that you started to wake up to reality, they did the only thing they knew how to do - they love bombed in tandem with the loss of all inhibitions. There was almost nothing they were not willing to do or let you do to keep you as a supply. When you reflect on it, the things they said they would never do, or only do with you, or told you that you were the first, they made sure they gave it to you and did it really well. Remember, the gesture was some grandiose thing. They may have thrown the party of the century, they may have given you some rarified sex, they may have given you some money, they may have given you the world and everything in it. It was all to hook you as supply.

Another method the narcissist may employ is the Savior/Satan method. This occurs when the person that causes the hurt is also the one who sooths the pain; the one who tried to drown you is the one who throws you the life jacket; the one who set you on fire is the same one to put the fire out. The narcissist gets off on making you mad and provoking reactions.

Getting you out of character is a turn on for them; that is why make up sex feels so good. It offers them a negative form of supply. You are likely to develop Stockholm Syndrome with a person who has a sick pleasure of seeing you become sick.

Normalize not forcing people to choose you. Let people do what they want so you can see what they'd rather do. If they think they can find better elsewhere — let them. Respectfully.
-Pammy DS

Right now, I'm stuck somewhere between what if, what might, and what could have, and what never will and all I want to know is what actually is.

~Christina Hart

CHAPTER 10

NARCISSISTS AND LOVE

The million-dollar question for those suffering or recovering from C-PTSD of narcissistic abuse is, "Did the narcissist ever love me? They said they loved me. There were moments when they demonstrated love to me." So, was it real? Or was it all an illusion? Perhaps the more important question is, are narcissists capable of love? Love is pure intention in action. Narcissists, however, are relationship chameleons. Their focus is, "What about me?" They do not love. They cannot love. But they can attach and play the role of someone in love.

They mirror you and reflect to you a version of you from themselves that you are looking for. You are only seeing bits and pieces of you and others from their past that they like and reflected. They blend in to all that is surrounding them to appear to fit in, and when in a new relationship, they do the same there as well.

To a narcissist, love is an external source of validation used to boost their self-esteem. They do not understand that real love involves reciprocity. Instead, they believe that love is something they can obtain from a person or object and use to feel better about themselves.[17]

— KETAN PARMAR, MD

One of the most common misconceptions is that a narcissist loves themselves. However, the truth of the matter is that they dislike themselves immensely. Narcissists know they leave a lot to be desired. They know they are lacking in a lot of areas and attempt to overcompensate in other areas to diminish the fact that they are deficient. This is why they present a false self for someone to love.

Narcissists may show you love and act in loving ways, but this tends to be conditional, in that displays of love depend on what you can give them in return. For people with NPD, relationships tend to be transactional. Love requires compromise. To a narcissist, compromise to a certain point becomes surrender. Their losing control or not being in a position to manipulate is like a fish being out of water. Eventually they will suffocate but before they do, they will find a backup supply.

Narcissists operate with pride, ego, and shame avoidance. The narcissist operates in the shadow self and behind a mask.

---

17   Arlin Cuncic, MA. Medically reviewed by Sabrina Romanoff, PsyD. Can a Narcissist Love? : It's hard to love someone else when you lack empathy. https://www.verywellmind.com/can-a-narcissist-love-7112051 taken 12/22/2023.

After suffering narcissistic injury, they feel betrayed and think that holding themselves accountable on any level is not an act of love. As a matter of fact, they are provocative victims and refuse to be held accountable by the person they are doing the things to. So, since you held them accountable, it feels like an attack and not love.

To them, it feels like you are punishing them for making them be honest and acting with morality and integrity. After all, they are in survival mode, and when one is surviving, being moral goes out the door to preserve life. The first law of nature is self-preservation. They never leave this state of being to compromise; ever. Love is not self-serving, proud, boastful, exploitative, jealous, manipulative, controlling, overbearing or envious.

A relationship — whether romantic or platonic — with someone who is diagnosed with NPD can be toxic, drama-filled, and in some cases, traumatic.[18] 1 Corinthians 13: 4-8a reads, Love is patient, love is kind. It does not envy, it does not boast, it is not proud. It does not dishonor others, it is not self-seeking, it is not easily angered, it keeps no record of wrongs. Love does not delight in evil but rejoices with the truth. It always protects, always trusts, always hopes, always perseveres. Love never fails.

The amorous narcissist is likely a hopeless romantic filled with nostalgia. They will likely rehearse in your ear all the good ol' days stories. They may live in the moment, but

---

18   https://psychcentral.com/disorders/can-a-narcissist-love#narcissism-and-love Taken 2/26/2024

to keep you blinded by the inadequacy of now. They mention the scattered good days of the past. In doing so, they only bring up the past to use as a weapon.

They are so selfish; they cannot genuinely care for anyone but themselves. Even their concern for others is predicated on what they can get out of the relationship.

What appears to be confidence is merely a cloak of lies and insecurities. That mask of self-flattery, perfectionism, and arrogance is a cover for the self-loathing that they will not admit. Only the self-aware narcissist will look at themselves and try to adjust their behavior. All the other types are likely too afraid to look within themselves with self-reflection, because this would mean they would have to admit they were wrong. In the mind of the narcissist, they are never wrong. To admit that truth of being wrong would be devastating to their ego. As far as the self and love go, they do not have much of an actual "self" at all. This is because they clone people they meet and steal desirable traits from them and mirror or project them to others.

As this relates to emotions, they are dead inside. Love is not an emotion to them. Real love is a choice. They can pretend really well to be emotional, but no actual emotional evidence is there. They appear to be crying but they have no tears. They may give an expression of shock, but they are pretending. They may give the appearance of disgust, but this may be hidden jealousy. Do not make the mistake of thinking their narcissistic rages are them expressing their actual emotions and concern. They may have realized that they lost control of their victim and that they now have to figure out their next steps quickly. The rage is only an attempt to get validated to some degree. Their insatiable unfillable appetite for validation makes them sad because they are unable to appreciate genuine love, and in contrast they will alienate or isolate anyone who shows genuine love.

Narcissists do love, but not in the sense that normal people love. Narcissists who fall in love shower the person of their admiration with much affection and smothering. In the beginning, things are a dream come true with them. They may give or gift you with so much stuff it blinds you to their ulterior motives.

They hover and watch closely to make sure no-one is encroaching on their territory without their permission. Their giving is phony too. They are likely getting the resources from someone else to give to you. However, they may work at this, and then gaslight you later with an, "After all I did for you..." line. In relationships, people make sacrifices. That comes as standard with any relationship, but the narcissist hates to their core sacrificing, compromising, and giving without getting an immediate return.

Some studies suggest that the narcissist is incapable of love because they do not even love themselves. Therefore, how can they love someone when they do not have self-love? Their love is predicated on 'what you can do for me?' If you cannot offer supply to them in some way, they will not have any dealings with you other than superficial ones. For example, if you were good supply, they love you for the things you provide.

If you ever cause them to feel insecure with your providing, they will quickly secure a backup plan for the future. They are distrusting of genuine love, so struggling financially is not a desirable thing for them. In other words, romance without finance is a nuisance. With the narcissist and love towards them, there is no in-between. Either you love them the way they think love is, or it is not real love.

In many instances, narcissists do not deem themselves as capable of being loved. They punish you for loving them as it highlights their differences. They are likely angry because authentic love is one thing they cannot mimic from you. They feel defective, unlovable, and run from the truth. They are running from themselves and cannot escape, because they are always with themselves. In their early developmental stages they were either over-praised, abandoned, abused, neglected, or undervalued by the people who were trusted with parenting them.

Human beings are said to be creatures of habit, reliving their childhood as adult age people. This makes them seek love, or what they think is love, in all the wrong places. They may seek it everywhere from grade school to high school, to college, graduate school, careers, jobs, clubs, and organizations. They must move from place to place and person to person to avoid discovery and detection that they are inadequate as a person. As they develop a relationship with you, they have a "get them before they get me mentality."

They are distrusting of everyone so they may do something self-destructive that will alter the dynamics of the relationship. It is only after they do this that in many instances, they realize they jumped the gun and realize their partner genuinely loves and cares about them. But what can they do about the past? Perhaps blame shift and guilt trip to avoid accountability.

They probably have already done a dishonorable, deal-breaking deed which, if discovered, would embarrass them and likely break the trust and the relationship up. They must keep the secret. The secret is an ego stroke and a gentle prick at their guilty conscious. The secret and lack of trust in others is what is killing their relationship(s). But they do not trust others, and are driven by their feelings of pleasure. Therefore, all of their relationships are pleasure-seeking opportunities.

You may be wondering why the narcissist chose you. A good analogy to explain the mate selection process for a narcissist is to think of the narcissist as an engineer. They are attempting to create a relationship paradigm that will support their extremely extensive and abnormally delusional psychological needs. What they ask and want of you may not be detailed in print, but they will expect you to read their minds and provide what they want.

The narcissist's perceived needs are so great and deeply rooted in childhood trauma being triggered that they have been forced, for the sake of psychological survival, to figure out which types of people can and cannot meet their needs as supply. They also seek who will and will not put up with their erratic behavior, temper tantrums, and distorted set of relationship rules. Those who can tolerate them, they keep.

Those who they cannot manipulate, they deem as difficult and discard. Below are a few points to note about narcissistic love:

◊ A narcissistic person's "love pattern" will generally predict how they will behave in a relationship.

◊ A romantic narcissist is in love with the idea of being part of a "perfect" couple. When flaws are revealed, they see no point in staying.

◊ Nostalgia will bring a romantic narcissist back to a previous partner briefly, but they will likely leave again.

Nobody falls in love faster than a narcissist that needs a new place to stay. Their constant need for validation, supply, and staying behind the mask of their "false self" causes them to seek to relocate frequently, to hide from the possibility of being discovered for the fake they are. They change partners frequently. They may even have multiple lovers they vacillate between while in a so-called monogamous relationship. This is called monkey branching.

One would think as vain as they can be that they love themselves and others. But they present themselves as a false narrative to everyone. The person you were experiencing was an empty shell of a person that has mastered the art of pretending to be a cluster of people they favored, playing manipulative games all in one body. They deserve an academy award for the role they play and the lengths they go to in order to acquire and secure supply. Their biggest care is for supply, not really you.

When the narcissist tells you, "I love you!" it is a delusional lie. Do not believe it. The truth is, they may love how you make them feel. They may love what you do for them. They may even love how you make their image appear to the public. But their love is transactional. If you are not doing something for them directly or by proxy, they will discard you or have nothing to do with you at all. Furthermore, how can you love someone when you do not love yourself?

Their saying "I love you" is nothing more than love bombing you. That is their feelings for the moment talking. The dopamine rush is giving them the sensation that this is a wonderful experience. However, they do not know you well enough to be so in love that early in the relationship. There is such a thing as love at first sight but think about it. Have they spent quality time getting to know you well enough to say, "I love you"?

They loved you about as much as lions love hyenas. Can they tell you your favorite color? Can they tell you your favorite food? Can they tell you your favorite genre of music? Can they spell your whole name? Probably not. But they are so in love. You are actually competition to them. You just have not detected it with clarity yet. They want to beat you, control, and dominate you, not love you. Their love for you is phony as a three-dollar bill and worthless as a counterfeit four-dollar bill.

Their love is superficial at best. Narcissists are not capable of loving you properly, because they only see you as a potential supply for long-term or short-term gain. Their lack of empathy also halts the love tank. No empathy, no sympathy, no love, all in one person. If for any reason you demonstrate that you are not willing to be their doormat and let them use you up, they will unleash a cycle of hateful behavior that can leave you confused. Violence, then request forgiveness with the promise to never do it again. Then blame you for the violence.

Then later repeat the same offense. But they claim they love you. They may cheat, hide it, and never admit to it. Why? The lie suits their interests. They may want both of you and if they admit to infidelity, they will definitely lose you. The other person probably does not know about you. But if they do, the narcissist has them feeling so good about stealing love that they are blind to the game being played on them too.

So they omit information, lie, gaslight, and blame shift for anybody discovering their infidelity. But cheating is a choice. They chose the person. They chose to take the conversation that way. Chose a time and place. Chose to travel there. Chose to engage in the activity. It was not an accident. It was deliberate and intentional. But do people who love you act that way? No one who loves you would ever risk losing you with actions that are deal-breakers. But a narcissist would.

Let us be clear, you do not love the narcissist because they have presented a false self for you to love. You love the cloned illusion mirrored to you in the form of a human body. They were wearing a mask and pretending with you. Their false self is a conglomerate of different people they have studied and mimicked to give a perception of a person to fall in love with. They are, at best, an avatar. The person you have does not even know who they are. They have been pretending so long that they cannot tell you anything but the rehearsed lies they have been successfully getting away with in the love bomb phase of their relationships.

I hate to be the one to tell you, but the person you fell in love with probably does not exist. What you may have experienced with the narcissist is a little bit of the mimicked qualities stolen and projected to you. They may have had ten relationships. Out of the ten, they took ten different people's attributes and presented them as their own to the next relationship.

The narcissists were, at best, a character in a play. It is likely that you fell in love with your reflected self which the narcissist was mirroring back to you during the love bomb phase. In the love bomb phase, they were telling you all the things you desperately wanted to hear. They were running game on you. They were painting a picture of an ideal situation for you and them. The narcissist was merely reflecting your own wants, wishes, desires, and good qualities back to you in order to snare you.

You talked about God; they talked about religious things along with you. You liked traveling; they probably talked about places they would like to travel to. Coincidentally, they just happen to be the same places you want to go. When you talked about certain foods, they discussed the side dishes that go with those certain foods. Let me say here that the honeymoon phase, or love bomb phase, often means you let your guard down. This is especially because it seems so good and so true. In fact, it almost seems surreal. Too good to be true. Anything that is too good to be true is usually a lie. Just as fast as they lured you in with the agreements, they switched up on you and left you confused in their duality. Most of the things you like, they echoed you on it. After doing so, they later switched. They changed their mind and no longer want those things.

The things the narcissists love about you are also the things they later hate about you as it reflects how ethically poor they are. They love how intelligent you are, until you are intelligent enough to figure out the games they are playing. They love how you speak up until you speak up to them on their mess. They love your confidence until their devaluing no longer works to tear it down.

They love how financially stable you are until it is exposed how financially irresponsible they are. They love your morals, until you establish boundaries and they have to stop being amoral. They love how things work out for you, but will get irritated after a while because you make it seem like magic and their self-sabotage blows up in their face when they try to do things. They may love how you save the day, until you save the day and get the admiration and credit that they felt they deserved. Their love is fake and most of their life is the result and their own karma returning to them. Furthermore, accountability is Kryptonite to the narcissist. I want you to remember, love without accountability is an act of manipulation.

The narcissist disrespected and lost respect for you because you loved them unconditionally. To them, this is absurdly ridiculous behavior. No one else ever loved them that way. Therefore, they concluded that you are trying to run a game on them. In their imagination, you are plotting to do the same thing to them that they are plotting to do to you and others.

They see you putting up with their cheating, triangulation, goldbricking, disrespect, lies, manipulation, condescending behavior, and self-destructive ways as weak. The truth of the matter is that you must be strong to love people for who they are and not what they do, even though they lied the whole time from the day they met you until the day they discard you. You must be strong to love people in spite of their ways.

You must be strong if someone has to spend their time trying to break you down. You must have good esteem for someone to constantly badger you to bring it down. You have good qualities. That is why the narcissist wanted you in the first place. They needed you. You never needed them. Furthermore, this is all the more reason to hate you. You are doing an amazing thing, waking up to the delusion and getting liberated. Again, if you did not have any good in you, they would not have stayed as long as they did. No one breaks into an empty house to rob it and no one values fool's gold.

That is why, when the narcissist gets love, they have a tendency to walk away from it because they do not have the capacity for the compromise that love brings. The narcissist has a delusional perception of what they know love is, so they want what they think is love. The love, tolerance, and compromise that you gave to them. They said that was not loving.

They said you trying to help them grow is not love. To them, it is judgement on a perfect person who can do no wrong. Who established that standard because real love rebukes. Real love corrects wrong. Real love does not feel good at first, because it changes what most people want to remain the same about them. The goal of genuine love is to become the better version of who you are like. People can love someone the way they are, but should motivate them to want to be a better version of themselves.

The only competition in love should have been, 'how can I out-honor this person with respectful behavior and gestures that create a good space for both of us to be the best versions of ourselves?' The other person should be able to help you see parts of yourself you are blind to that need attention. But narcissist cannot accept this, because it would mean that they are wrong. Instead of being happy that someone noticed something that they thought was fine but was not, the narcissist suffers narcissistic injury and seeks revenge. Love is and always will be a choice - a choice to do what is right, even if one does not feel like it, but recognizes that something needs to be done.

The narcissist is a transactional being whose only modus operandi is figuring out 'what can I get out of being in a relationship with you?' That alone disqualifies them for love.

I think it's safe for me to tell you here that they were never true to you. EVER. At best, they intermittently cheated and entertained their other supply. It was not every day, but almost all the time they can get away with contacting and meeting with them, they did it. How droll. Stop! Think! They've probably had affairs more times than they've made financial deposits for the future they are faking they want with you.

The narcissist knows very well that if a higher bidder comes and things get rough for you long-term, they are playing both sides or will be out altogether. Like a thief in the night, they are gone, but if conditions become unfavorable with the new supply they may return like a boomerang when you start getting back on your feet. But remember; they don't care one way or the other for anything but securing supply. It's not love. It's the thought that this feels awesome and thrilling and if it changes, they will find that feeling again. It is certainly not them feeling they will commit and sacrifice or be inconvenienced without exercising a backup option all while faking that they love, honor, cherish, respect or truly care about you.

PERSON WITH NARCISSISTIC TENDENCIES

◊ Exhibits one or a few traits (e.g., believes other should admire them)

◊ Behaviors come and go, or are only present in some situations (e.g., only at work or school)

◊ Life and relationships not affected in a major, negative way; traits may even give an advantage (e.g., help them succeed at work)

◊ May be developmentally normative in childhood and teen years.

◊ Can recognize traits as negative and be open to changing them.

◊ Has/develops self-awareness and insight.

◊ Can be empathetic but may not be at times[19]

---

19   https://www.verywellhealth.com/narcissistic-personality-disorder-types Taken 12/7/23

PERSON WITH NARCISSIST PERSONALITY DISORDER

◊ Traits are fundamental to their personality

◊ Behaviors are constant across situations

◊ Traits significantly impair their life, making it impossible for them to have healthy relationships

◊ Does not see traits as negative and is less likely to be open and willing to change them

◊ Often lacks self-awareness and insight

◊ Has little to no ability to empathize; may "weaponize" empathy and can even be sadistic[20]

An octopus and an orangutan can fall in love, but where would they live? They are both intelligent but from two different worlds.

~Doc. B

---

20   Laura Dorwart. Medically reviewed by Steven Gans, MD. *7 Types of Narcissism. Covert, grandiose, and other types of narcissistic personality disorder.* https://www.verywellhealth.com/narcissistic-personality-disorder-types-5213256 taken December 7, 2023

CHAPTER 11

THE DUALITY OF NARCISSISM

If the phrase "damned if you do and damned if you don't" had a character type by it, the narcissist would be the poster child for it. Let me start off right here saying, the narcissist, in their mind, is always right. Even when they are wrong, you are not right. They have a unique way of spinning things to go in their favor. You can try to win an argument with a narcissist, and you will frustrate yourself because they are always right even when you show them proof that they are wrong. They believe their lies and are convinced of the version of reality they created with that lie.

Therefore, you will discover they are antagonistic. You can be their ally yet they are so distrusting of anyone that they will challenge you when you are indeed in favor of them. They may use word salad to say a bunch of nothing when you ask them a direct question and want a yes or no answer.

Furthermore, you may find yourself in an argument even when you did not disagree with some point of view with them.

Duality is defined as an instance of opposition or contrast between two concepts or two aspects of something.[21] Synonyms include doubleness, duplexity, ambivalence, dichotomy. Often, narcissists put victims or their supply in a double bind. They are notorious for this. They place the victims in contradictory scenarios where the victim will be led to a negative outcome in the end. In the end, the victim will be blamed or fail and be filled with anxiety due to the manipulation the narcissist is giving.

The narcissist may demand that they prioritize them. The narcissist will then accuse the victim of being too clingy. When the victim lightens up, the narcissist then says they are not attentive. The narcissist will accuse the victim of wanting sex too much. Then when the victim lightens up, the narcissist accuses them of cheating or not wanting them anymore. The narcissist may demand that the victim be supportive of their dreams or aspirations.

When the victim tries to express that they do not disagree but thinks that a better choice can be made, the narcissist accuses the victim of not being supportive. Even if it fails, the narcissist will blame the victim for agreeing with them in the first place when they knew better than the narcissist.

Narcissists are constantly locked in a state of duality. They are diametrically opposed to you at all times, even when you have their best interests at heart. It is as if they have a

---

21   Https://languages/OxfordLanguages.oup.com taken 1/13/2024.

split personality. From day to day, you often wonder 'which version of this person will I get?' They want power, but no responsibility. They want to be left alone, but not abandoned altogether. They want to be needed, but not relied upon as a source.

They want something for nothing without doing the work to earn it. They want the grand prize, but not the process it takes to earn it. You will discover everything they want, and desire is a contradiction. You probably have walked on eggshells, hoping that you do not trigger them or say something that will make them explode. You have probably rehearsed something in your head ten times before saying it to them, only for them to disagree or argue with whatever you chose to finally say.

They vacillate between being hot or cold, on or off, good or bad, happy or sad, up or down, broke or rich, with it or not with it, and all or nothing at all. For every solution you find, they can create a new problem especially since they are experts at **goalpost moving.** They are so committed to winning and being superior to you that even if you agree with them, they will change their answer to a more detailed answer just to one-up you. They are control freaks, and love to believe they are experts in their domain.

They are always right, which makes you wrong all the time. This is part of their delusions of grandeur. Yet, in so many ways, they are self-destructive, self-loathing, self-sabotaging, selfish people. This behavior can make you feel crazy and develop brain fog. Why? Because they rewrote history right in your face. They recall things that never happened and question you about it and you do not remember it because it did not happen that way. To them because you do not remember, you do not care. But you cannot remember it that way because it did not happen that way.

But they have you questioning reality even if you recorded the events and watched it in playback. This keeps you confused. Again, from day to day, you do not know which version of them you are going to get. One morning everything was good. The next morning everything was bad, and you are the worst thing that ever happened to them. One day you are the best thing that ever happened to them. The next day you are so full of flaws that you can never seem to get anything right.

One day you need to live a little, meanwhile if you do and things go wrong, it is your fault. One day, they love you flaws and all. The next day you are the bane of their existence and make them the most miserable. When you meet and get to know someone who is a narcissist and are remarking to yourself how extraordinary they are, remember that they are two-faced – under the sway of a dark duality that controls all of their thoughts and actions.[22]

Narcissists will oscillate between feelings of superiority and inferiority. Either everyone loves them, or everyone hates them. Everything is amazing, or everything is fucked. An event was either the best

---

22 https://thenarcissistinyourlife.com/cruel-duality-of-the-narcissistic-spouse/ taken 12/31/2023.

moment of their lives or traumatizing. With the narcissist, there's no in-between, because to recognize the nuanced, indecipherable reality before him would require that he relinquish his/her privileged view that he/she is somehow special. Mostly, narcissists are unbearable to be around. They make everything about them and demand that people around them do the same.[23]

When you are dealing with a narcissist, nothing is exactly black and white. A narcissist is a walking contradiction in human flesh. They are extremely selfish and persnickety. There are few things, if any, that truly satisfy the narcissist. You can give them the world, and everything in it, and they will say you did not include the moon.

You can buy them a house that is a fixer-upper, they will complain about making the repairs. You can win the lottery and promise them half, and they will tell you why they deserve more than half. Narcissists do not know what they want so they project that onto their victims. Narcissists love to win arguments at all costs, even if their point of view can be proven against with factual evidence. You can show them documented proof and they will still argue to win and be right.

These victories are called Pyrrhic victories. It is the kind of victory where so much energy is placed on winning, you lose the respect of your opponent to get the victory. You

---

23   Mark Manson. *Everything is F*cked: A book about hope.* HarperCollins Publishers. Broadway, New York. 2019.

can be right, or you can be happy. You do not have to argue with them. You do not have to be in competition with them though, unbeknownst to you, they are secretly in competition with you.

When it comes to relationships, coming to a mutual understanding is supposed to be the most desired outcome. Not with a narcissist though. It is like flipping a coin and them saying, "heads I win, tails you lose." to every flip of that coin. The word salad, deflection, and need to be right is undeniably unbelievable with them.

If you get in a relationship or situation-ship with one, you will find yourself in a constant fixed state of duality with them. If you catch them cheating on you, they will never trust you again because you caught them. Read that again. The same narcissist will probably get the best night of sleep they ever had knowing that they cheated and got away with it.

They get an almost euphoric high from having their spouse and their lover in the same room, and the one they are supposed to be faithful to not knowing. For them, it is not so much the act of cheating, but the opportunity to be sneaky and hide information and getting one up on you makes them feel special. They feel that you are capable of returning the favor. Since they feel you are capable, they will never let you live that down - all because you caught on to the fact they cheated on you.

They will tell you, "It's kind of your fault I am cheating on you." What a gaslighting statement. In their mind, if they imagine you can do it, then you will eventually do it to them.

To them, if it was easy for them to do and you are so calm, you probably are cheating too.

There is a common theme that runs through marriages with narcissists. "What is mine is mine and what is yours is mine. I am entitled to it because you changed my status." This is the strong outer image that the narcissist has created which convinces everyone around him that he/she is a delightful, charming, caring human being–someone who goes out of his/her way for others and is extraordinarily successful at the same time. Everyone on the outside looks up to these narcissistic wonders, asking themselves, "Why can't I have this polish, charm, and self-confidence.[24]"

The narcissist conceals a duality beneath the ingratiating compelling smile—the Shadow. In his/her private life, the narcissist is unveiled–fully revealed. Narcissists are deceptive, craven, venal, exploitive, explosive, manipulative and completely lack empathy. If their wives and children could speak, they would tell you stories that are hair-raising. The narcissist is a dictator in his home.[25]

It does not matter what the narcissist has attained professionally. He/she can be highly educated, remarkably successful, or non-educated and unsuccessful, rich, or poor or in between—they are still a narcissist and have a fixed personality disorder that does not change. More people need

24   Linda Martinez-Lewi, PhD., LMFT. The Narcissist in Your Life. https://thenarcissistinyourlife.com/cruel-duality-of-the-narcissistic-spouse/ taken 12/31/2023.
25   Ibid 12/31/2023

to speak up about the total series of hells that narcissists put their families through. It is an ugly moving picture. [26]

Narcissists are most psychologically violent to their spouses in particular. At times they are physically violent as well. Most of them get away with this savage treatment because the non-narcissistic spouse is too afraid and doesn't feel that they have a voice of their own. It should be noted that some of those who marry narcissists were treated cruelly in their childhoods, and have continued this expectation in their marriages.[27]

A narcissist may say you never include them in the decision-making process. Then, when you do include them, they yield to your decision making only to criticize the decision and go against it because it may require adjustments for them. After agreeing to your face, they will "change their mind" or usurp your authority. They may even rage to get you to change your no to a yes. Then they will criticize any mistake you make.

They become persnickety, meaning petty and trivial about insignificant things. They want you to have the memory of an elephant for the good they did, but the patience of Job for the mistakes they made. The same narcissist will forget what you told them minutes after you speak to them. They do not care so they do not pay attention yet at the same time, want you to remember and remind them of all things that go in their favor.

---

26   Ibid 12/31/2023
27   Ibid 12/31/2023

Every word you speak, move you make, or decision you stick to it is an unwanted, unasked for critique. However, they cannot accept constructive criticism as this feels like an attack on their character. This can be particularly challenging when you are attempting to express areas that you feel they can change/adjust for the better in. Where there is no change, there is no growth.

They are stunted in their growth. At best, they are teenagers with toddler mentalities trapped in adult bodies. Toddlers make a mess and come to a more mature or capable person to ask them to clean it up. Someone else has to clean up the proverbial mess and change the proverbial diaper. They know it but hate to admit it because they want to escape the shame associated with being so low in mentality after aging year after year.

If communication is key, being understood unlocks the door. They say they want you to communicate but stonewall you, overtalk you, interrupt you, or become dismissive when you are making points that go against what they want to do. The child trapped in the adult body cannot understand what is best for them. This is problematic for them, because they want to project themselves as perfect while knowing they leave much to be desired.

Covert narcissists, as the name suggests, are more subtle in their manipulative and abusive tactics. They will hide their superior and grandiose delusions by putting on an act of being nice, humble, caring, and shy. However, when their buttons have been pushed (i.e., when they experience a narcissistic injury), their true colors start to show. Similar to other types of narcissists, they may explode into rage and yell, hit, or throw things, or stonewall you and act like you are entirely insignificant.[28]

The narcissist may tell you of some grand idea, then dry-beg you for the money or resources to support the idea. They do not have the plan together but want you to sponsor and fund it. By dry-begging they do not have to ask a direct question. It gives grounds for you, the empath, to help, because that is what you are accustomed to doing. There may come a time when you do not agree; they will say you never support any of their ideas and always reject their ideas. The words never and always are extremes and absolutes. They can trigger responses.

If you help them, the duality here is that they never asked you. Again, this is called dry-begging. They hinted and made comments in an attempt to get you to willfully volunteer to help. You did and they will plainly say, "I never asked! You volunteered." Even with that, narcissists are like Janet Jackson's 1980s album single, *'What have you done for me lately?'* It could have been yesterday, a week ago or the same day. They will say, "Why are you mentioning old stuff? You still on that?" Thus, they avoid responsibility and accountability for their actions.

---

28   Stoeber, J. (2014). *How Other-Oriented Perfectionism Differs from Self-Oriented and Socially Prescribed Perfectionism.* Journal of Psychopathology and Behavioral Assessment, 36, 329-338.

You may tell a narcissist your deepest fears, desires, fetishes, traumas, family secret or privileged information and then tell them not to tell anyone. The narcissist is guaranteed to use this information against you in an argument, or during the smear campaign or even the discard stage of the relationship.

They swore by heaven and earth to never reveal your deepest information and as quickly as you gave it to them, they explode and embarrass you by telling your information or even posting it on social media. Then they will claim, "You never told me not to tell anybody!" or, "I did not think it was so important!" According to Maria Consiglio as it relates to narcissistic abuse,

Narcissists base your character on the way you react to their abuse. If you fight back, then you are abusive. If you do what they did to you, you are vindictive. If you show them the way they have been treating you, then you are petty and childish. The only reaction the narcissists wants is blind acceptance. They could say and do whatever they want, and you have to let them without opposition. If you do not react the way they want, then you are the cause and reason for the conflict.

Narcissists may talk about killing themselves. This is an attempt to get attention. Most people who want out, check out. They will cry out for help but are likely not to tell you exactly that they want to kill themselves, because they do not want to end up committed. A narcissistic parent cannot afford to lose their children as supply so they may avoid counselors, therapists, and social workers. On the other hand, they may see the counselors, therapists and social workers and lie with a straight face and make themselves appear to be a misunderstood angel when in fact, they are a devil and wolf in sheep's clothing. It should be noted here that the narcissist believes their lies, so they may beat a lie detector test with ease.

To try to describe narcissists to people who have not encountered narcissists is challenging. Being in a relationship with a narcissist is like being a comedian with your own personal haggler. They are capable of driving you to the point of giving up. Then, they start complaining about the fact that they made you exhausted enough to give up in the first place. It is like damned if you do, and damned if you don't. You can never get it one hundred percent right with a narcissist. They goalpost move.

As soon as you think something is good enough, there is more to do. I am reminded of a Peanuts cartoon. Lucy used to love to pull the football away just before Charlie Brown could kick it. Charlie would swing his leg at the football and Lucy would snatch victory from the jaws of defeat. That is what being with a narcissist is like. You have every duck in a row, and they will sabotage the plan and leave you frustrated. They may take the savings it took years to acquire and spend it on some hair-brained idea that is going to fail. If you get upset, you do not love them. But if you, do it to them, it is the end of the world.

The narcissist feels it is free game to criticize you but on the contrary they are hypersensitive to your feedback. A narcissist will gaslight you by saying you are not communicating with them and that you are the problem. But they do not listen to you fully. They present themselves as though they are excellent communicators. However, there is more going on here than meets the eye.

The same narcissist that accused you of not communicating will withhold information as though it gives them the power to share it with you later. They may cut you off while speaking, stonewall you, and be dismissive of your contribution to the conversation. What others do not see is how, when you share your information, they use it and weaponize it against you. Thus, having your information revealed makes you shut down.

The narcissist will tell you important things at the last minute, saying they forgot and do it in a joking but condescending way. Telling you at the last minute is designed to back you in a corner. They may even mention the fact that you are not forthcoming with information either, to try to hide that they are trying to manipulate you. Understand that they probably set the whole scenario up. Yes, you read that right.

They know you have a heart of gold, and they have a heart of coal. Their scenario was all designed to wait until the last minute. In the smear campaign they can attempt to paint you a certain kind of way if you say no [which they hate]. They may have overextended themselves and cannot manage a fiscal responsibility. They will come with a sob story and beg or even bargain with you to get the thing they want. They may need a few extra dollars to complete it, and please – say that you do not have it and see how quickly that duality comes back. You are the safety net; you do not have it and they do not have the exact same thing but are defiantly desperate to point out that you do not have it either.

Furthermore, rules, exceptions, and regulations apply to you, but not to them. As noted before, you may have told them something private and asked them not to tell, but what did they do? They told it. This makes you apprehensive about sharing more information.

In your mind, you may be thinking, 'If you did it once, you will do it again…' Or, you may be thinking, 'past behavior is a good indicator of future behavior…' Yet, the narcissist will gaslight you about withholding information from them to seduce you into sharing more information, only to take that information and build a case against you in the devaluing stage of the relationship. While attempting to converse with them, you may notice they will cut you off while you are in mid-sentence and not allow you to fully express yourself.

Saying things like, "Ooh, let me say something." "You never let me talk!" "Are you going to control the whole conversation?" "When do I get to talk?" "Is this whole thing about you?" "You're not letting me talk." "How is any of what you are saying fair?" The narcissist is very dismissive about your thoughts and opinions. They are not listening to understand; they are listening so they can interrupt the conversation, avoid accountability, deflect, and maybe at best ignore you, all while giving the appearance they care. In the same token, they will say that you never told them anything. How could you express a full thought when they keep cutting you off? After a while you realize that they are trying to steal your voice from you. Do not let them.

Covert narcissists, unlike overt ones, will often use self-deprecation to play the victim. They might say things like, "I'm such a horrible person, you deserve better." Or, "You'd be so much happier without me." These kinds of statements are meant to make you feel guilty or compel you to defend yourself and your love for them – playing straight into the narcissist's hands.[29]

Next, a narcissist may complain to you or their friends about money. The duality here may be that they either want complete control of the finances, or they want nothing to do with the fiscal responsibility so that when things go wrong, as life sometimes will, they can avoid all accountability and/or blame you for either your or their lack of involvement. They may tell you to quit your job and that they will pay all the bills.

This is a trap. This will give them control of the finances and allow them to manipulate you because they know you have basic needs too. They will be so intoxicated with power that they will deny you the very oxygen of love and then, in a

29   Stoeber, J. (2014). How Other-Oriented Perfectionism Differs from Self-Oriented and Socially Prescribed Perfectionism. *Journal of Psychopathology and Behavioral Assessment*, 36, 329-338.

grandiose gesture in front of others, be very benevolent with the same money they keep from you. They may be living off credit cards. Unbeknown to you, they pay one card off with the other card and keep the rotation going. It is clever, until you find out about it, and they max out the cards and need a little help from you.

Now they are upset that they must ask you for anything - why? Because they want to be independent of you. They want to grow up so badly but again, they are a child trapped in an adult body. They want to branch out from you. But life caused them to need you. You remind them of all the qualities they wish they had by nature. The narcissist may be a gambler. Their gambling addiction may be so strong that they have no problem with using their earned money and then taking your earned money, promising to give it back. If they win, they may give you the money back, but with a verbal string attached. You may get some type of gaslighting, manipulative, or smirky remark instead of thanking you.

The narcissist feels entitled, so they never want to owe anyone and not get something out of the deal. However, if they lose at gambling, they will get upset with you for having the nerve to ask for what they agreed to give back. When you ask for anything back, they will instantly deflect to some time when you needed them or a situation in which they did something for you, in order to guilt trip you and thus they avoid accountability again. This is known as leveling. Accountability is Kryptonite to the narcissist.

The narcissist may say things to you like, "You never tell me, so how am I supposed to know?" "You always make it about you like you are in the relationship by yourself." "Why are you the only one with money? I need money too." "If you would just listen to me, we would be in a much better position." "You are always hiding money!" [It is your family's emergency fund that both of you know about] and you are looking at them looking like an adult yet throwing a temper tantrum like a toddler.

Which is another duality. They are children trapped in adult bodies. At best, you are looking at a person who may have stopped growing up mentally as a teenager, but their biological body aged and their knowledge about some things increased. Their narcissistic rage is like watching a three-year-old fall on the floor in a store.

They cry, scream, beg, promise, slam doors, move furniture, throw things, and the whole thing was done to get their way. Being with them is like being in a parent-child relationship where you are the parent, and they are the rebellious teenager who wants their independence. They know enough to do things on their own but are dependent enough on you to still have some needs from you too. This also is part of their resentment of you. How dare you be more mature than them and have the skills and answers they do not have!

Some narcissists may be poorly educated while others are very educated. If poorly educated, they may become intimidated, irritated and even anxious around others who have achieved what they should have, would have, could have but never did. Remember - they are projecting a false self and must project this at all times. However, fake people can only pretend really well until reality shows up. You may notice the narcissist can talk about things with clarity. However, they are parroting what someone else said and they probably cannot tell you the source of the information.

The very educated narcissist is egocentric and may lord over you that they have so much more education than you. They may be part of various clubs and organizations to help hide the insecure self. They may have more degrees than a thermometer, but no job because they are a career student. This narcissist is an overachiever.

They may be the CEO, CAO, COO, CFO, head of the club or organization, director of activities, leader, coordinator, pastor, or coach, yet they cannot stand people. The uneducated narcissist will gloat when you make mistakes as an educated person. It gives them a rise to be able, as a less-educated person, to know something you with your degrees do not know.

Another duality with the narcissist is when they hear you talk, disregard what you say, and then they listen to someone else say the same thing but they apply what they said. This is a very frustrating experience as they already do not listen to you without interrupting your thoughts, yet someone else will say the same things and they will listen, implement, and apply those things. The unmitigated gall and audacity. I hate to be a bad news bear here, but they know what they are doing. They do not respect your words and thoughts. This is why the narcissist disregards your words. But here is an amazing twist. The narcissist, though they cut you off, listened just enough to take the exact words they did not want to hear and will project your words to someone else as their own. The narcissist knows you are making good sense, but it hurts them so badly that it is coming from you. They make several demands but seldom, if ever, reciprocate. Even when they do, it comes with something attached.

One thing is important to note - the quality of how they treat you during the relationship is hugely dependent on how many options the narcissist has. If you are the best option, they will treat you slightly differently and with a little more value. However, if they have other options and some of them could potentially replace you as the new supply, they will discard and even reverse discard you. They will not care what you think, say, find out, accuse them of or anything else. Basically, you were an itch that got scratched.

Simply put:

1. They can be outwardly charming but hellish at home.

2. They can be thin-skinned but thick-headed.

3. They may obsess over their image while undermining yours.

4. They may be reputation-sensitive but superficial.

5. They may be entitled while depriving you simultaneously.

6. They may be combative and defensive at the same time.

7. They may be self-righteous but amoral in their relationship.

8. They may be emotionally demanding, but clueless to your needs.

9. They may seek constant validation but ignore you emotionally.

When you are not in alignment, there is duality. When you are in alignment, there is non-duality.
~ Richard R. Phahlawi

Children do not "take sides" with the better parent or parent they love more. Children "take sides" with the parent they have learned it's safer to agree with. Remember that.

~ Unknown

CHAPTER 12

NARCISSISTS AS PARENTS

Fredrick Douglas once said, "It is easier to build strong children than to repair broken adults." Narcissistic parents have unreasonable expectations of their children.[30] An example of this was observable in the parents of JonBenét Ramsey as they paraded the American child beauty pageant winner through several beauty pageants. She was the winner of five prestigious pageants - two in the state of Colorado, and three around the country. JonBenét went on to take home first place titles at Little Miss Colorado, America's Royale Miss, and National Tiny Miss Beauty. Her mother was a former beauty pageant winner herself. JonBenét's father, John, had reservations about the child participating in public displays of the pageant culture. Unfortunately, JonBenét, at age 6, was found brutally murdered in the basement of their home

---

30   Emily Standley Allard. *14 Signs You were raised by a Narcissistic Parent.* https://www.msn.com/en-us/health/other

in Boulder, Colorado. It was alleged that her parents were responsible for her death. Later investigations and evidence suggested that an unidentified male suspect was responsible for her death. Perhaps the parents were living vicariously through the child and pushed her too hard. The murder has never been solved to this day.

A goal of parenting and healthy marriages should be to foster an environment that is safe and conducive to the personal growth of each individual within the family unit. However, there are dynamics that play out when dealing with a narcissistic parent. Parents with narcissistic personalities tend to be relational antagonists who act in a way that is compulsive and which undercuts others. Undercutting others serves to gain them a sense of control and sense of superiority.

The narcissistic parent may create chaos and trauma where there is not a need for any. Narcissists do not co-parent, they counter-parent. Narcissists are in petty competition with their partners, children, and everyone else they have the semblance of relationship with. The narcissistic parent is the toxic person and most broken person in the family system. The narcissistic parent, as the most mentally unhealthy, mentally unstable person in the group, writes all the rules and defines all the roles.

And as long as the family complies and lives out the roles they define, which can change as the narcissists sees fit, then there is peace. It's passive-aggressive peace. It's dysfunctional peace. It's predicated on you not triggering them. But, as long as they are seated on the throne and have absolute rule, everything is good until they are triggered.

As members of a functioning society, perhaps we would not like to admit that parents are capable of behaving badly towards their children, but the fact of the matter is that there are parents who abuse, neglect, traumatize, triangulate, invalidate and misuse their children. Narcissists are the exact kind of people who can hurt the most vulnerable ones in the family - their children.

The abuse can be overt or covert. It can come in the form of dog whistling or yelling bellicose ravings in drunken rage. The stages of narcissistic abuse are love bombing, idealization, devaluation, discarding, hoovering and repeat. Most narcissistic parents with multiple children favor one or more over the others. The children can feel and sense this. They feel the favor over the scapegoating.

They can sense when one child is the favorite, and the other is getting little-to-no love at all. Even when narcissistic parents are shining an idealized light on someone, this is nothing more than a form of manipulation. Today it can be flattery and praise. From the same parent comes criticism and blame mixed with goalpost moving.

These behaviors often make the child become codependent as they seek the validation of the parents. But the narcissistic parent will likely never validate the child, because they are trying to manipulate and control the narrative. All the flattery and praise today can turn on a dime and end in judgement and contempt. The child will be stuck trying to win the affection of a parent who will not let them know that they are worthy of love, validation, praise, and are special. But since the narcissist knows they are not special, they do not want to run the risk of telling someone else, especially their own child, that they are special. Why? Because they are jealous and envious of everyone around them. Jealousy is when someone wants what you have. Envy, on the other hand, is when someone does not want you to have something. Narcissistic parents are both jealous and envious of their own children.

Good parenting requires unselfishness, compromise, empathy, compassion, and a willingness to see your needs as secondary while the children are of the age that requires more attention from parents. These are traits that a narcissist does not have. Narcissistic parents will have a challenging time allowing their children to gain a sense of their own individuality as a person or get their needs met.

Needs like feeling safe in the skin they are in, security, attention, emotional support, education, structure, health care, and quality time. The narcissist will know the child needs these things and deny the oxygen of love to the child, and have the audacity to say to them, "I did the best I could." With a narcissist, they use people, and if you have not guessed it, they use their children.

A narcissistic parent will have a challenging time allowing their children to become independent of them. The idea of the child growing up and living their own life is scary, especially for the aging narcissist because they are looking to secure some long-term supply. The toxic methods used in raising the children may give the appearance that they care about their children; however, if the child gives a hint that they could threaten to interfere with a steady supply, the narcissist parent may abandon their child, emancipate them, kick them out with no plan for their future or even trade the child off for supply of some kind.

On the other end of the spectrum the narcissistic parent may wear the mask well enough to hide behind bragging on social media posts or supporting their child's extracurricular activities. That same narcissistic parent will be so toxic that the child will seek their validation and approval and become a people-pleasing perfectionist. The child may become a narcissist themselves. James Baldwin once said, "Children have never been good at listening to their elders, but they have never failed to emulate them."

The narcissistic parent may see the child[ren] as a meal ticket. So, the narcissist may resort to having multiple children by a sports athlete, upcoming music mogul or someone with plenty of money as a means of securing a lifestyle they cannot maintain on their own with their own resources. The narcissist can goldbrick and live off the earnings of the child support payments, and breadcrumb the child with money designed to support them and assist with their upbringing.

Let us say here that the child of the narcissist is a prodigy; talented and gifted in many areas. The narcissistic parent will induce tiny amounts of venom into the psyche of the child to guilt-trip the child into doing things for them. They will be the child's biggest cheerleader in rigorous extracurricular activities. They may screen the people the child dates because they may threaten the big payday the parent is waiting for.

The parent looks like they are looking out for their child, but the modus operandi is to secure supply at all cost - even at the expense of the child having a childhood - if it means they may miss future supply. A narcissist will abandon their family and reinvent themselves. The narcissistic male and female cannot sustain an authentic relationship in a marriage or as a parent.

They act out, become triggered easily by the child's needs or rage, and have multiple affairs, mistresses, girlfriends, boyfriends, secretly on the side and out in the open. They are doing what they feel is best for them. They have no shame about their destructive and reprehensible behavior. Both spouses and children suffer because of this.

You may not be able to detect the signs of a narcissistic parent; however, there are some tell-tell signs. Below is a list of thoughts the narcissistic people display to their own children:

1. **They expect the child to be their caregiver when they get older**

Most children look to have their own independence by the time they become adults. They grow up and leave the nest and start their own families. However, with a toxic narcissistic parent, they plant the seed at a relatively immature age that their child has to take care of them. This often extends well into adulthood, where the narcissistic parent can be very condescending and manipulative. A common line might be,

"If it wasn't for me, you wouldn't have what you have." Or ,"As much as I did for you, you owe me."

2. They put their needs first above the child[ren]

Prioritizing needs is something parents learn to do. Narcissist parents have a sense of entitlement. They expect and may even demand that their children make sacrifices for them, so their wants and needs are accommodated.

The child has a life too, but the narcissistic parent expects the child to drop everything and cater to their every whim. This gives the narcissistic aging parent a sense of superiority over their child. The same narcissistic parent will demand that the child does things for them, and then the same parent will miss things like graduation ceremony, weddings, induction ceremonies and have excuses as to why they could not make these events.

3. They have poor boundaries in the children's life

Narcissists hate boundaries. Narcissistic parents especially hate boundaries their children establish. They can be very intrusive and probing with questions about how much money someone makes or saying things that are inappropriate for them to even mention. They may intrude in the marriage, or counter-parent the other parent's authority. They may undermine the spouse of the child they have. They may also inject venom in the people in the adult child's circle.

They may mention some embarrassing childhood traumatic experience and share it in a way to smear the character and credibility of their child. This behavior may leave the child feeling self-conscious.

4. As parents, they are emotionally reactive, but shame and guilt trip the child for displaying emotions.

A common trait of narcissists is they are often angry and aggressive when they feel disappointed or frustrated. They often feel that way. If they perceive their child as being critical of their behavior or defiant, the narcissistic parent will attack physically or verbally. These reactions often manifest as yelling, sudden fits of rage or, in more severe cases, physical violence or breaking things.

When the child expresses their emotions, the display of emotions can make narcissistic people extremely uncomfortable. As a reaction, the narcissistic parent may develop contempt for the child. They may shame, guilt-trip, and insult their child into not sharing their emotions at all with phrases like, "Get over yourself, it wasn't that big of a deal," or, "Stop crying all the time and toughen up." The reaction will be that a child will grow up not knowing how to express their emotions because the narcissistic parent has taught them to suppress their emotions.

5. They have a golden child and a scapegoat child.

At the core of the narcissistic <u>personality</u> is a split between the ashamed and vulnerable interior self (which is usually kept repressed from consciousness) and the special (superior and entitled) exterior persona. Narcissists as parents typically project this inner duality onto their children, seeing one as an extension of their idealized self and another as an extension of their repressed shadow self.[31]

---

31 https://www.psychologytoday.com/us/blog. Taken 3/26/24

Narcissistic parents use triangulation and play favorites with their children. The game is to manipulate each child to seek to be the object of the parent's affection or recipient of praise and admiration. The child may even seek to be affirmed by the narcissistic parent. The golden child will receive praise, compliments, and rewards. The scapegoat child receives the blame, criticism, and disapproval for ninety-five percent of what they do.

The golden child/scapegoat cycle makes children feel uncomfortable, psychologically unsafe, and disloyal. Psychologically this may cause the child to think they need to go along or impress the narcissistic parent to avoid the bellicose ravings, rages, and avoid walking on eggshells to maintain good standings within the family unit.

6. They place blame on the children and don't taking accountability

Narcissist never think they are wrong. They try so hard not to feel shame that they have the need to feel perfect. When the toxic narcissistic parent makes mistakes or errors in judgement, they avoid accountability of any kind and shift the blame on to their children. The behavior is subtle but often stings emotionally, and the damage is done internally.

Common refrains from narcissistic parents might be something like, "If it were not for you, I would have money. You are expensive." "Between going to my job and you, I have no time for me. You are the reason I am so tired." Or, "I could go get a better job if I didn't have to do for you and your siblings."

Eventually children of narcissistic parents learn to internalize these comments and begin to self-blame, self-gaslight, and believe: "I am a burden and cannot do anything right. I am in my parent's way."

7. **They view their child as a source of supply for their validation**

Remarkably similar to a reverse smear campaign, the narcissistic parent sees their child as a tool for their supply. The child is an extension of themselves when they are away from the parent. In more cases than not, the narcissistic parent has checked out and almost abandoned the child even while in their presence. The narcissistic parent is detached and disinterested in their child privately. They generally invalidate their child's need for connection or validation.

On the other side of the spectrum, the narcissists will often loudly flaunt their children publicly when they score the winning goal or get the big part in the school production. You might see them constantly bragging on social media or bringing up their child's beauty or talent in conversation. But the same parent is only using the child to make themselves seem to be a good parent when they are not good at all.

8. **Neglecting to teach them basic life skills**

By not teaching the child basic life skills, the child is more dependent on the parent for guidance. The narcissist is likely not going to teach the child life skills unless it gives them praise. They do not want to empower their growth, confidence, and sense of independence. Often, they will become extremely critical of their children, causing them to develop difficulty coping as teens and young adults.

9. Manipulating them financially

With a narcissist, what's mine is mine. And what is yours is mine. The narcissist can go one of two ways with this. Most people see money as a tool. The narcissist is likely to use it for control and manipulation. They will probably use gifts, payouts, and in the future fake the promise of inheritance - reminiscent of the dangled carrot in front of the donkey that he never reaches. They may also see their child as a walking ATM. Whenever they want money, the child is to blindly give it to them, even when they have responsibilities of their own.

10. Coddling their Children

Narcissistic parents bail out the golden child excessively as they are the favored child. This comes as an extension of the narcissist's sense of special entitlement. The child could develop stunted growth in learning how to develop life skills. The narcissist will use the fact that they helped the child as a method for manipulation, Often gaslighting and manipulation them with, "I did this/that for you."

11. Abandoning them in their time of need

The opposite end of coddling, the narcissistic parents may abandon their child physically or emotionally in times of vulnerability and genuine need. The narcissist already does not care unless it affects them directly to provide some type of supply. The child may develop abandonment issues, such as separation anxiety while younger, and as an adult tolerate unseemly behavior.

12. Conditioning the child to normalize Shame and Rage behavior.

It can be quite traumatizing for the children of narcissistic parents to live in an atmosphere of rage and shame. Each day the child is yelled at, raged at, and spoken to in a way that does not create inner peace and feelings of security. The child may grow up feeling this is normal and seek relationships that are toxic in nature. Cortisol levels in the body heighten when faced with stress daily. Long-term hyperactivity interferes with healthy development and can cause chronic and acute health problems such as high blood pressure, chronic fatigue, exhaustion, weight problems, lack of motivation and brain fog.

13. Punish, Dissent and Reward Compliance.

Narcissistic parents tend to reward compliance and blind obedience in their children with praise and privilege, and they will punish any opinions that go against their ideal thinking. The punishment can come in the form of invalidation, judgement, fits of rage, bellicose ravings, breaking things, detachment, ignoring the child and rejection.

14. Cheating on the child's parent with open malice

Narcissistic parents will serially cheat privately and openly. When seeking external validation, they may cheat and let the child meet the lover under the auspices of another name to hide the detection. The narcissistic parent may say that the paramour is their personal trainer from the gym, my work friend, or dance partner. They may say 'this is my special friend'. When narcissists think they have found someone to replace the spouse, they cheat in the open. They hide in plain sight.

They may cheat in their spouse's face and ask the child to go with them and expect them to turn a blind eye to infidelity. The narcissist is always the victim in their story. The excuses for cheating may be: their spouse works too much; they are lonely; they are bored; they need excitement; they are being neglected; and they feel they are missing something. Lovers are designed to eventually take the place of the spouse in all areas. The child is left in the middle of the infidelity, feeling torn between both parents.

15. Adultifying them before their time.

It is not uncommon for narcissistic parents to push their children or even grandchildren into the roles of an adult to meet their own needs. The exploited children may function as adults. The youth may have to work like an adult, pay bills/rent, run errands like an adult, oversee business like an adult or even do things around the house that adults usually handle. They may also become the therapist for the adult, analytical people, nurses, spouse substitutes, sexual conquest, and best friends of these narcissistic adults.

In a worst-case scenario, the child will develop Stockholm Syndrome and sympathize with the abuser and may be involved in some unsafe, unfair, or illegal activities that can cause adults to get arrested, if discovered. The child is literally forced to abandon childhood innocence, adolescences, and become a convalescent in adulthood, chasing a childhood of which they were robbed. The child will likely become triggered easily once they become an adult when they relive or encounter scenarios that mirror the trauma.

The child of the narcissist will likely become an adult that is dependent, codependent, a perfectionist, a people-pleaser, put others' needs above their own, very accommodating, overthinkers, overachievers, obsessive-compulsive, hopeless romantics, passive for fear of rejection, more tolerant of inappropriate behavior and indecisive with decision-making. All of this has likely come from the parent causing them to feel inadequate.

The sign of great parenting is not the child's behavior. The sign of truly great parenting is the parent's behavior.
~Andy Smithson

CHAPTER 13

NARCISSISTS AND SEXUALITY

Sex is not a reward and should not be used as a weapon to punish - ever. But a narcissist will likely use sexuality for both. Withholding sex and intimacy from your spouse for prolonged periods of time is harmful. Sexual avoidance can lead to confusion and resentment. A sexless relationship can lead to break up and or divorce. The malignant narcissist gets a rise out of withholding from their partner and may do so to provoke a response. The covert narcissist might use sex bombing to secure a new supply. Sex bombing includes giving the new supply the best sexual experience they have ever had.

When the target is driven by their loins and not their intellect, a narcissist can hook them with sexual gratification of lust. Because narcissists do not know what love is, they also use their sexuality for pleasure contracts. It may appear to be a union of love. But it is nothing more than a pleasure contract

DR. BYRAM MCKINZIE, SR.

which will get broken when the narcissist feels the simplest slight.

Sex should be a sacred, enjoyable discovery between two individuals. The narcissist will turn sex into an exhibition for multiple partners. Because relationships require obligation, commitment, compromise, and accountability to someone, they usually just keep multiple partners or become someone else's side piece. Interestingly, they would sleep with someone else's spouse for years and pray for a faithful spouse for themselves. If that is not a backward-walking giraffe.

Most narcissists do not view sex as normal people view it. Narcissists see sex as a means to keep someone tied to them. Narcissists also see sex as means to secure supply. When starting a relationship, the narcissist may have sex right away to see how sexually compatible you are to them. Sex with a narcissist is a kind of supply utilized to stroke their fragile ego. They may love bomb you by telling you, "Nobody can do it like you," "You are the best I ever had," or "You'll never find another like me to do the things I do."

If you study the narcissist long enough, you may realize that sex is all they have to offer. So, they do what this author calls sex bombing. Much like love bombing, they put sex on you in such a way to attempt to control and manipulate you. If you are led by your loins, the narcissist can get you hook, line, and sinker. That is why it is so good with them. They pull out all the stops and tricks to hook you. But take sex away from the equation, and you will soon discover they have little to nothing else to offer at all.

Whoever said, "You can't turn a whore into a housewife," was probably referring to a transactional narcissist that uses their sexuality for reward. The idea is that since a whore is accustomed to exchanging their sexual favors for money, they will likely not stop even when they get married. The hypergamy causes people with narcissistic personality disorder to sell themselves to the highest bidder since they live in survival mode.

If their grade A supply fails to provide, they will seek new supply quickly. This is highly typical behavior for the female narcissist. The male narcissist is likely addicted to pornography as he is detached and does not know how to make meaningful connections with people. This will be covered with more information in the section, Male and Female Narcissists.

According to Dr. Umar Johnson, emotionally damaged people are always sexually promiscuous. If the amorous narcissist is emotionally damaged and traumatized, they need constant validation from others. Sex happens to be the means to get someone to say yes. If they were abandoned, neglected, or abused by people who were supposed to take care of them, they must entertain someone else to fill that void. They need someone else in their personal space.

Next, **It is not yours, it is just your turn.** It, meaning anything including their body, sexuality, resources, time, efforts, and situation-ship. They only like you for the convenience and availability of you. Once your availability was gone, he or she was able to replace you easily. The separation anxiety they likely experienced growing up caused them to be detached and they can move on with ease. The narcissist was addicted to presence and validation. Once you stopped supplying that, he/she replaced you.

A narcissist is almost always grooming a new or next person, even when with someone solid in their lives. Some narcissists love to cheat. It is the thrill of doing something exciting and almost getting caught that motivates them to do the cheating. It is the fact that they are doing something to you that you may suspect but are not sure about which makes them excited. They seem almost aroused to cheat in close proximity with you and their lover.

They will have them come to your house, sit in the same room, eat at the table, go on group and business trips, and the list goes on and on. They also cheat to one-up you. Thus, they cheat so that if you ever cheat on them, it does not smash their already fragile ego. They already do not trust people - even loyal, resolute, and devoted people who have proven themselves are not trustworthy to a narcissist.

As a matter of fact, the narcissist is so distrusting of good people that they look at the good people as suckers. The amorous narcissist may use sexual supply to get even with you when you make them mad. Also, the sexual supply will be used for triangulation and transaction for goods and services when you tell them "No" to something they want or want to do. While some narcissists are serial cheaters, others will not physically cheat even if presented with a clear opportunity, but they will use people for triangulation as a means of manipulation to get supply. There are signs you cannot ignore with narcissists. Tell-tell signs of narcissism in sexuality:

◊ Making comments about hypersexuality.

◊ Often triangulates you and compares you with others from the past or current partners to make you compete to be better than them.

◊ Making subtle hints of additional people (threesomes/ orgies) involved in their own personal sexual escapades.

◊ Sex is an ace card to expedite transactional behavior (pay to play).

◊ Discusses pushing boundaries sexually such as trying new things that you may not do normally.

◊ They comment, "If I was to ever cheat...." Meaning I need a justifiable reason to do it.

Because the narcissist has so many previous sexual conquests from monkey branching, it is likely they have a sexually transmitted disease. One of their empty, soulless moves is to perhaps give you the disease and hope you stay with them. They are likely to pass it on to you and function as if they knew nothing about them having it, and blame you for passing it to them. They will know they have it, yet sleep with you and play the victim.

Now it is your fault for not using protection. They also have problems being with one person - because they have made so many connections with their body, it makes it difficult to be with one committed person. Loyalty, commitment, sacrifice, and compromise are things narcissists are not likely able to give nor willing to be able to do without immediate withdrawal.

Usually, they move on before anyone can figure out who they really are behind that mask and façade of sexual conquest. What they may deem as love is actually lust in action. It is lust because the narcissist gets a rise out of punishing you. They are in love with the idea of you as the ideal sexual conquest. However, like all things they have, they will get bored and seek new gratifications for their lust. This is an easy move for the narcissists because they have likely had more partners than the number of years of their age, but less meaningful relationships as they have fingers on one hand.

Do you think it is love they are feeling? It is not love but lust which they are feeling. The lust has layers of deviance. The narcissist will probably tell you they have never done this or that before. This may be true, but if it means they can keep you as supply, they probably will try it with you.

If it is tolerable, they will keep doing it even if it goes against their grain because it keeps the supply available. Remember, anything they do is for them and not for you. They must get some return on the investment, or they will likely not participate as it costs them too much on their end.

Many sexual narcissists are more than likely perverts. Their perversions are layered. They have layers of deviance. Most are addicted to pornography. With so many genres of it, there is seemingly an endless supply. Porn does not ask them to express emotions or demonstrate empathy. Porn does not say no and allows them to view others uninhibitedly, and they get to practice their detached behaviors which allows them to not have to emotionally invest themselves in another person. Studies suggest their porn viewing is accompanied with chronic masturbation. You could literally be lying next to them naked or in something sexy and they will masturbate to porn, rather than rolling over in the bed and engaging in sex with you.

This behavior happens because the narcissists has classically conditioned themselves to avoid rejection. They do not want to risk hearing "no" for an answer. Also, their addiction to porn can get bad enough that they cannot get aroused without the use of porn. They may pay for it online, have stashes of it on their computer, or have created some with former lovers.

They may have tapes, DVDs, and recordings of you or former lovers you know nothing about. Please understand, all addictions are real. Since sex feels so natural and there is no one to tell them no, they indulge when their person tells them no. Then try to practice what they have seen on you or their other supply. If you are kinky, they will mirror all you want but hate and resent you for having to do it with you to get the supply they want because they feel a sense of entitlement.

Again, with porn, the narcissist can observe and study others' behavior and then practice some of the acts on their suppliers. For males, they get to avoid possible rejection from their partner. For females, it may stem from them trying to please their partner. Since they are experts in manipulation, they will probably ask you or convince you to get into decadent activity from pornography with them. As long as you agree with it and are willing to participate, they are okay.

The day you say "no" to their advances, it is a problem. Expect guilt trips, insults, shaming, and coercion to try to persuade you to see things their way. Some of their pornographic behaviors turned common to them may include coprophagia, urophagia, urolagnia, emetophilia, bestiality, necrophilia, BDSM, sadomasochism, bondage, pegging, anilingus, cunnilingus, fellatio, pandering, threesomes, orgies, swinging, open marriage, role play, sex toys, cross-dressing, and other activities.

Some narcissists are so deviant they would ask you for sexual favors, get you to agree, then record them without your permission and try to use the recorded data against you to extort and run a smear campaign on your character. Again, any attempt to say no to their advances will likely begin a cycle of guilt-trips, shaming, and begging to get you to agree. The narcissist does not know how to manage rejection. Their fragile ego cannot take it. To not get their way is a loss of control. They desire control at all costs.

Remember their desire is a calculated, and a deliberate attempt to start the assassination of your character. All of this was done to triangulate you with others they may see as new supply. They may use the information of the activities against you in a smear campaign once you begin to say no to other advancements. They will resort to bullying, threats, threats of abandonment, threats of exposure, intimidation, and extortion for personal gain.

Please understand - the narcissist will treat the new supply differently than you, but they will go through the same predictable stages with them too. You may have begged them to change, adjust, or do something differently and received zero results. However, for the new supply, they will do all the things you desired and desperately wanted. The new supply is not different or more worthy than you. They are simply different or new. The narcissist is using manipulation as a tool to fuel, gaslight, or cause you to respond.

It is also good to note here that while with a narcissist, as it relates to sex with them, "it" was never yours. It was just your turn with them. Remember, their thinking is, 'what's mine is mine and what is yours is mine'. No matter how much they may seek to convince you that you are the only one, there is always someone they have in a secret relationship with you know little to nothing about.

With social media, the narcissist can always find new sex partners, sneaky links and keep up with their ex and the next, all while in a relationship with you. They will attempt to present a red herring and confuse you. But pay attention. They will start echoing and parroting things the new supply says and does. They will start doing things with you they learned from the new supply; some new moves, if you will. Thus, you discover they do not care about you like normal people care.

You are there for supply, sex, and resources. You happen to be the object of that desire for now. The person they are cheating on you with is there for supply. They do not care about them either, beyond supply for the stroke of their overinflated ego. All the people they triangulate are there for supply. Never believe that you are special or exclusive to them. Nobody is as single than a narcissist in a relationship already. Their constant need for validation will keep them ever searching for endless supply partners. They are a bottomless unfillable pit with an insatiable, ineffable appetite for external validation. Their unspoken motto is, 'if you cannot offer me assistance, you need to keep your distance'. Trust and believe that their social media friends are followers of past, future, and current potential supply.

A narcissist can be in a polyamorous relationship or open marriage where they and their spouse are supposed to share an understanding. The narcissist will become selfish and greedy then find a reason to be sneaky and hide what is beautiful and open yet break the trust of their partner. They do this because they are self-centered, self-seeking, pleasure-mounding people.

Why sneak and cheat or hide things when you have given them the freedom to be open? Why hide when you do not have to? Because narcissists love being sneaky and feeling superior. Doing things out of your sight gives them a sense of arousal in that they know something you do not know. This so-called secret gives them perceived power. The narcissist will change names in their cell phone to pseudonyms or not save the numbers just so they can be sneaky. Nobody is as single than a narcissist who gets married to their steady Grade A supply.

Nobody cheats more and triangulates more than a narcissist who views people as optional verses essential to growth. Why? Because they have an insatiable appetite for pleasure and admiration. Their cheating is not about cheating, but rather about external validation and self-aggrandizement. They only care about you in the sense that you will remain a good supply. The day you disagree or have a change of heart is the day you will receive insults, shame, and the need to be right flooding your hearing. Below are seven reasons the narcissist cheats.

1. They lack morals and are insecure thus they need to prove to themselves that someone besides you desires them.

2. They are ego driven and self-serving and do not care how you feel (unless you will end as their supply) or what it will do to you to find out.

3. They do not believe you will leave if you discover the infidelity. Their arrogance makes them feel that they are too smart for you to catch on or that they can charm you into forgiving them.

4. They do not believe the hidden life is any of your business. Remember, it was stated earlier that no one is more single than a married narcissist. They don't believe any of what they do privately is your business.

5. They lack integrity overall. They cheat in love, business, school, socially, their family, and in life period. Thus they believe no one should stand in the way of what they want.

6. They shift the blame. As part of their delusion, they convince themselves that you did something worthy of them deserving to cheat. They became unhappy and now they feel you owe them the latitude of at least cheating to make up for the unhappiness.

7. Unbeknownst to you, they have emotionally detached and broken up with you in their minds and are living like they are single. But one minor detail they deliberately forgot is they want to come home because the new supply does not have it together and they need to come home until the supply can do it all.[32]

Remove sex from a relationship and you will discover that a lot of people have nothing else to offer.

~ Tom Hardy

---

32 Women's Empowerment post paraphrased "Seven reasons the narcissist cheats"

A crowded mind leaves no space for a peaceful heart.
~Chrisine Evangelou

"If you're trying to preserve a relationship with a narcissist, the best thing to do is set direct limits and stick to them."
~Aimee Daramus, PsyD

CHAPTER 14

ARE YOU THE PROBLEM AND THE SOLUTION?

This chapter is a question. Are you the problem and the solution? Narcissists are delusional creatures. In many instances they leave you confused. You do not know whether you are coming or going. You are not sure if things are good or if they are about to go into a narcissistic rage. Narcissistic people are spectacular at finding a way to shift the blame and accountability onto others. They have a unique way of justifying their problematic behavior and avoiding any responsibility. To a narcissist, you are both the problem and the solution. You may think you can communicate well with them by telling them how you feel.

They hate to be bothered and inconvenienced. You, in their eyes, are the problem, and they want the noise to go away. So, they blame shift and deflect. This is gaslighting at its finest.

When there are issues in the relationship, no matter how big or small, they will be unable to effectively communicate with you to resolve the issue. While you are an individual that can consider others' feelings and make changes based on the needs or yourself and others, the narcissist is incapable of these same behaviors.

It can be maddening to be in a relationship with a narcissist because you always feel like you are the problem, and nothing ever gets resolved. Remember; you are likely not the issue and, in the absence of the narcissist being better able to connect with others through empathy, and without their willingness to accept their own faults, you will continue to feel like you are going in circles during discussions with the narcissist.[33]

You may have had an experience like this - the narcissist accused you of something but for some reason they cannot get their act together. It is referred to as casuistic formula. If this, then this. Examples include:

◊ You work too much. If you had been home, then I never would have cheated on you. It is your fault I cheated on you.

◊ If you would just listen to me, then none of this would have happened.

◊ If you had just given me an allowance, then I would not have to ask others for money.

---

33 Emily Mayfield. *Why are problems never solved with Narcissists?* https://www.mindsettherapyonline.com

◊ You are such a stick in the mud. If you would lighten up a little, then things would not be so dull.

◊ If you would just let me be myself, instead of trying to change me, then we would be much happier.

Please understand that as long as you are in a relationship with a narcissist, you are somehow to blame for things being the way they are for them. You are the bane of their existence and if you just changed for them, things would work out. Sorry to tell you this but a narcissist is a self-sabotaging, self-destructive, negative-karma-catching imbecilic fool.

Simply put, you are not the problem. Yes, the two of you together are toxic. Oil and water are both liquids, but they do not mix. Yes, you have some responsibility to the acceptance of some of the self-inflicted pain you are in. But you cannot control their actions. You can only control your actions and reactions.

Stating the problem + offering a solution + adding the consequences = the narcissist will (hopefully) hear what you are saying.

CHAPTER 15

THE "N" WORD.
WHAT HAPPENS WHEN YOU TELL A NARCISSIST NO!

Rejection is a pretty universal experience and the fear of rejection is very common, explains Brian Jones, a therapist. Most people are accustomed to being told no about something. Often in general conversation, people ask yes and no questions. But what happens when you tell a narcissist "no?" If you reject, disagree with, turn down, argue with, or tell the narcissist "no!" get ready for an explosive display of a temper-tantrum-throwing-child trapped in an adult body creating a narcissistic rage. A simple "no" from you is a very powerful punch in the gut for the narcissist - it exposes them to feelings of shame from which they then do not have the tools to disarm themselves.

Dr. Emily Mayfield, APA Psychologist Mindset Therapy PLLC in Montgomery County Texas, recorded video detailing what happens when you tell a narcissist "no." Much of what she discussed is detailed here in this section. To understand why a narcissist seems to fall apart mentally when you tell them "no" you must understand what character traits make up the narcissist, and more specifically someone with narcissistic personality disorder (NPD).

The traits commonly seen in people with narcissism include a sense of self-importance and grandiosity. They are preoccupied with fantasies of success, power, or intelligence known as delusions of grandeur. The narcissist believes that they are special or unique in some way and can only be understood by people of equal status i.e., talent, resourceful, connections, education, social status, economic status, business status, etc. These are usually their flying monkeys.

Narcissists require copious amounts of admiration, they feels entitled, exploit others, lack empathy, are envious of others, or feel others are envious of them while showing arrogant behaviors. The aforementioned are several different traits to consider in someone who might be a narcissist. However, an easy way to summarize those traits is that they involve a sense of superiority, and the narcissist is self-focused on how they are better than others and others cannot compare to them to maintain this inflated sense of self-importance.

They lack empathy and cannot take the perspective, logic, reason, constructive criticism, and opinions of someone else. Because they think they are never wrong and no one else is right, the narcissist thinks that their perspective, logic, reason, constructive criticism, and opinions are better than everyone else, and they cannot handle it when you tell them "no."

"No. You are not right."

"No, I don't have it."

"No, I do not want you anymore."

"No, I am not going to give you the seed money for the business."

"No, I am not having sex with you after you cheated."

"No, I don't want to talk about it."

"No, I do not want to participate."

"No, I do not want to have a baby with you."

It is important to mention that narcissists live on "supply." For them to function, they surround themselves with individuals who will focus on them and admire them at all times. It is crucial for them to be the center of attention whenever possible.[34] When you tell them "no" you are not only saying that they are wrong in some way, but to them you are also exerting power over them by not allowing them to do or have what they want. You are now their target and antagonist in the narrative they are creating. Constructive criticism means they did not do something right or that they have something to improve. But since they think they are perfect and right already, there is no need for criticism of any

---

34   Krisztina Petho-Robertson, M.Ed., LPC. *How Does a Narcissist Handle Rejection and No Contact.* https://upjourney.com/how-does-a-narcissist-handle-rejection-and-no-contact.

kind. Especially from you, as they see their way as superior to you and your way. You should just be offering blind allegiance to their already distorted reality they see as true. But you told them "no."

What will likely happen are a few things listed below after hearing "no."

◊ **They may immediately ask for your rationale.** Accepting "no" as a final answer is alien to the innate nature of a narcissist—they are essentially programmed to pursue their wants at the cost of everyone around them, so their initial reaction to being told "no" will likely be an intense campaign to find out *why*.

◊ **They may try to engage you in an argument.** Pushing your buttons and employing personal insults is a surefire way for a narcissist to try to distract you from setting a limit with them. When the verbal abuse starts to fly, you can rest assured they are trying to move you from your stance—and dumping some of their <u>anger</u> on you in the process.

◊ **They may alter reality.** You may find yourself faced with completely absurd "evidence" from narcissists as to why "no" is unfair. Narcissists are particularly talented at ignoring reality and making statements that are blatantly false—but they make them with such bravado that it will cause you to question what you know is real. This method, called <u>gaslighting</u>, is a very palpable way that narcissists control the narrative around them.

◊ **They may slander you to others.** When a narcissist cannot get what they want, demeaning you to others is a <u>defense mechanism</u> to falsely build up their <u>self-image</u>. It also helps them <u>rationalize</u>, in their own minds, why you're telling them "no" in the first place—if there is something inherently wrong with you, then your answer of "no" can be considered illogical and unfair.

◊ **They may try to woo you.** If the personal attacks fail to budge you, a narcissist often turns on the charm. Once the dust from hearing "no" settles, they may resort to future faking and pseudo-agreeing with you—but only with the hope that giving up a small battle will make you more likely to say "yes" the next time. It's all about power and control with a narcissist, so if emotional damage doesn't make you rethink your answer, they will likely consider <u>agreeableness</u> an option. After all—image is incredibly important to a narcissist, and they ultimately want to be viewed as the victim when you set a limit with them.[35]

Again, the narcissist is not okay with being rejected and told "no" because their fragile senses of self would be deflated and cannot take any sort of negative information that comes at them. If we say "no" to a narcissist, they will feel disappointed that we are not available to them at all times. They might not express their disappointment at first or in a direct way, but

---

35   Jamie Connon, MS, LPC. *What to Expect when you tell a Narcissist "No." How to predict the reactions when you to set limits with a narcissist.* https://www.psychologytoday.com/ March 6, 2023.

will instead wait for a perfect moment to punish us.[36] The narcissist thinks their ideas and decisions are flawless, and that to consider any other option other than what they suggest or propose leads to feelings of shame and then narcissistic injury. When the narcissist is told "no" they become defensive and go into self-preservation mode.

Their sense of entitlement kicks in and they almost stop at nothing to get what they imagine they want. When pursuing the things they want, they cannot allow themselves or others to think that they are not worthy enough or are wrong in some way. Again, this would mean they are wrong. In the narcissist's mind, they are never wrong, and you are never right. Because you have told them "no," you are their antagonist, you become enemy number one and are the target of their narcissistic rage.

The simple act of being told "no" for anything pops their delusional balloon and threatens their perception of narcissistic supply. They must quickly recover their lost supply before truly being exposed for the fraud that they are. The two ways a narcissist goes on the defensive and attacks the person that told them "no" are by either starting a smear campaign or engaging a narcissistic rage.

The smear campaign could be a reverse smear campaign. It is done to invalidate the one who harmed them since they now feel invalidated by being rejected and told "no." The rage could include yelling, throwing, and breaking things,

---

36   Ibid

slamming doors, making grand exits out of doors, threats, or even a physical assault of some sort to punish or strike fear in the antagonist who told them "no."

Although the smear campaign might be less obvious, it could be more long-term when compared to the narcissistic rage. A smear campaign is how the narcissist works to reinflate their narcissistic supply by painting a picture that you are crazy, they are the victim, and they are entitled to something that you denied them. It is a form of damage control the narcissist engages in when they feel like they are being exposed for who they really are.

[A fraud, a fake, a relationship chameleon, an imposter, a wolf in sheep's clothing, a doppelganger and a clone]. During the smear campaign the narcissist will paint you as a bad person and their chief antagonist in any way that they can. Their goal is to get the attention off them and their dysfunctional behavior and onto to you. The people they incorporate into the smear campaign may not even have anything to do with the reason you told them "no." By now you may have come to understand things with the narcissist often do not make sense, because everything is contingent on how it affects them and nothing else. 'What's in it for me' is the motto.

When told "no", the narcissist might also engage in narcissistic rage. The narcissist will become brutal, and their words and actions will go on the attack. They will name-call, yell, and belittle to feel more in control since the rejection sent them into a fit of rage. You have told them "no" and they attack to avoid looking awkward.

They must remove all attention from them and place it onto you. The narcissist cannot be told "no". Because of their fragile senses of self they are always on the defensive to protect against this low self-esteem and underlying awareness that they are not the superior person that they want you to believe that they are. Learn to say "no" without explaining yourself. It is a superpower.

No is a complete sentence. It does not require explanation or justification.

~Unknown

CHAPTER 16

NARCISSIST'S BIGGEST FEARS

There are a few things the narcissist fears. The two greatest things narcissists fear are being **exposed** and brought to **shame**. A narcissist would rather lose you or leave you than face the shame associated with being with you after being found out or being exposed by you and someone else. Shame is what the narcissist is trying to avoid. What shame, you ask? The shame of being found out as a pretender and imposter. They fear people will see them for who they truly are - nothing and nobody special. A petty hustler that is a day late and a dollar short who copycats people and uses catch phrases they heard to project this false self to the rest of the world.

They are an accountability dodger. An individual with an irresistible arrogance to be right and get their way all the time, at all costs. Narcissists will move from city to city to avoid being found out for the fraud they are. They will discard people if it means they can escape being exposed for things they actually did. They do not want people to discover they are the monsters in the relationships they are in. To keep their names clean, they may attempt a smear campaign to avoid any accountability. Why? Because it would mean they are wrong. And in the narcissist's mind, they are never wrong. Therefore, their amoral behavior is justifiable in their own mind's eye.

Next is that they fear that the spell they cast on you is being broken, and you are no longer going to be a good supply and blindly allow them to manipulate you. The charm and deceit are all smoke and mirrors and you are waking up and figuring things out. You were becoming a detective and working in espionage, and gathering data. You are Googling their behavior and coming to conclusions that something is just not right about this.

It is all becoming clear to you, and you are coming out from under the spell. The cognitive dissonance is wearing off. The Jedi mind tricks are not working anymore. The charm and words do not match the actions. Because they do not usually maintain lasting relationships, they can wear masks, mirror people, and run the game – you were figuring things out. But when they stay too long, eventually the mask slips and they make Freudian slips in conversation. They forget their own lies and let their guard down. They may tell you about a truthful traumatic experience from their past. But do not be fooled.

These are just confessions of their guilt and ways to get the negative supply of a reaction out of you. Write what they say down, because the story will change. Write the changed story down, because it will change from that too. They are an actor in a movie called *Life* and you are one of the starring roles, but you did not get the script. You are in a vicious game of duck, duck, goose, and you are the goose that lays golden eggs. They did not tell you that you signed up to be the leading role in a play called *Grade A Supply*. You are working for free. For them, it is the same script, different cast. It is lights, camera, action, now you are on.

Narcissists also fear missing out. They feel they are going to miss something by being fully committed and invested in a meaningful relationship with one person. They get bored easily. They feel that they must control everything so that they know exactly what is going on. This is to curate damage control. Damage control refers to the actions and strategies employed to **mitigate, manage, and recover from a crisis or negative situation.**

It is crucial in preserving reputation, minimizing losses, and restoring stability in various contexts, such as business and personal life. According to the Cambridge Dictionary, it also involves limiting the damaging effects of an action or mistake.[37] They need all the details, even if they are miniscule, because the details that are left out may be their doom. They cannot lose the false image they project and they cannot afford to lose their Grade A supply, especially if they are an aging narcissist. With the internet and technology, they have an almost endless supply of external validation. They keep

37   Surendra Kumar. Damage Control. EDUCBA/BLOG. https://www.educba.com/damage-control/

so many people available because their supply may end the relationship when they get tired of the phony person.

Since you know them well enough for them to have shared some secrets, they are afraid that you will do to them what they are plotting to do to you in the future. A narcissist may share a dark secret about themselves to take the sting out of being found out and embarrassed. By confessing, they are attempting to clear their consciousness, offer self-disclosure, and avoid accountability.

This also gives a false impression of honesty. They knew what they were doing; they knew it would hurt but they did not think about the consequences as they are impulse thinkers. They did not care about you because they saw you as replaceable. They are toddlers or teenagers trapped in an adult body. Their development is under arrest. Again, they would rather lose you or leave than face the shame associated with being exposed.

Love and respect – if they respected you, they would never hurt you. If they loved you, they should never hurt you. Women view love and admiration as proof you genuinely love them. Men view respect as love. But you can love a person very much and still not treat them right because you lack respect or boundaries. Thus, the narcissist will repeatedly say, "I love you," and still do stuff that does not align with the words. They do this because they are motivated by their feelings.

If they do not feel like it, even if it is the right, rational, reasonable, reliable thing to do, they are going to do what feels good to them. The feelings give them the rewards. And if it feels good to be contrary, they are going to be contrary. They are so self-centered that they do things like sabotage endeavors, counter-parent, goalpost move, pathologically lie, manipulate, cheat, steal, play the victim, intimidate, bully, and a host of other things that show they are literally control freaks.

These fears are fueled by the fear of losing control of the situation. They fear that they cannot control the outcomes in favorable directions for their benefit. They fear they are losing their sexual prowess and dexterity. They fear losing their good looks. They used to get the likes and DMs and other social media attention. They fear that they will lose all of their supply and validation and have to deal with themselves.

They fear being left alone, even if they are antisocial, because who would they have to practice their narcissism on and shift blame to? They also fear having to look inside themselves and see themselves for the ugly soul they are. That is not your fault, even though they will probably blame you or others for them being the way they are.

After getting invalidated by your narcissist for so long, you may start self-gaslighting and taking blame for their behavior. They are doomed. They know they are doomed but they hope that, against all odds, trying to control things will work out in their favor. But it will not. Lastly, they are trying to overpower you to the point of silence because they fear your spirit. They fear you recharging and regrouping and leaving them behind that is, if they do not discard you first. Trust and believe that they are discarding you if they find that you are not useful to their delusions. You'll notice this by all the petty comments and highly critical observations they make about you. Everyone is capable of making mistakes, but to have someone highlight your mistakes daily both verbally and socially is exhausting. Just know that they have found a new shiny toy and they are ready to let you go.

But they narcissist wants it to look like you were the one so them may result to reactive abuse and provoke you into action that leads to separation. They do not want to look like the bad guy. The shame is too much and that is one of their biggest fears.

Our deepest fear is not that we are inadequate. Our deepest fear is that we are powerful beyond measure. It is our light, not our darkness, that most frightens us.
~Marianne Williamson

People have a hard time letting go of their suffering. Out of a fear of the unknown, they prefer suffering that is familiar.
~ Thick Nhat Hanh

CHAPTER 17

WHO ARE YOU?

Who is the person in the mirror? I am about to tell you just who you are. You are an initiative-taking, conscious creature. You are a fearfully and wonderfully put together tapestry of human art in a body. You are eons of intelligence incapsulated into human form. You are spirit incarnate. You are radiantly beautiful. You are billions of cells in harmony and vibrational frequency aligned with creating space for you.

The world will ask you who you are, and if you don't know, the world will tell you.

- Carl Jung

Is your story with the narcissist a sob story? If yes, shame on you. You suffered. Yeah, you and about four billion others suffer - this life is full of suffering. You picked them because you saw something in them at one point. But if you are choosing to stay with someone who has checked out on you, then you are self-inflicting the wounds you are getting now. Why? Because you do not appreciate what life was attempting to teach you. You were supposed to learn to love and respect yourself. Life chose the person you cared about to pull it out of you. You were supposed to look within and validate and affirm yourself. But you possibly became codependent. You were supposed to reinvent yourself like a caterpillar does when it goes into a cocoon and becomes a butterfly. Then grow and have the best life possible so that your life is proof that you are more than a conquer.

You are an empath who likely has had a toxic relationship with a narcissist. You, as an empath, actually sense and feel emotions of others as if they're part of your own experience. In other words, someone else's pain and happiness become your pain and happiness. You likely put yourself in the shoes of others to attempt to see it their way.

However, you probably did not think about this - you are not in the skin they are in. You imagine you helped them by walking a mile in their shoes. But try being in the skin they are in. Their crisis becomes your emergency by proxy or default. You have become or are becoming a receptacle for responsibility. For example, you take your child to the county fair and let them play games for prizes. The child wins the large size prizes and have to carry them around the fair.

The child gets tired of holding the prize they won and begins to complain about how heavy the prize is they won. You come in and become their hero and take the burden of the prize they won off them and now they get to walk around free from the responsibility again all to win new prizes that are too heavy for them to carry. Shift that into adult relationships and voilà, there you are aiding and abetting the narcissist to do something and shift the responsibility on to you. They played stupid games and won stupid prizes.

Now they want you to carry the burden of responsibility now that the thrill of winning is gone and the responsibility of having to carry the load of the prize is there. But the narcissist loves to win and get new supply. Even a drug dealer will tell you never get high on your own supply. Stop carrying the load of someone else especially if they created the problem. I get it, you like to help and helping makes you feel good and seen. But they are using you. WAKE UP!

You love to be the suffering servant to the narcissist in your life. You are a **martyr**. According to Merriam-Webster dictionary, a martyr is a person who sacrifices something of great value and especially life itself for the sake of principle and a great or constant sufferer [victim for a cause].[38] As a martyr, you deemed it worthy that you become synonymous with your suffering.

You are so loyal that you would die for someone who would not uncross their legs for you and fix you a sandwich if they could avoid it. They would not cross a puddle for you but expect you to cross an ocean or sail the seven seas for them. When things go wrong for them, which they usually do, you are the savior safety net for them. You become inseparable

---

38   https://www.merriam-webster.com taken 4/17/2024

from the suffering because they convinced you to take the blame for their dodging accountability.

You are a perfectionist. You practice perfectionism.

Perfectionism is a constant and all-pervading feeling of never quite measuring up, never quite being or doing enough to please. To please whom? Everyone – yourself, others, and God. Naturally, a lot of self-belittling and self-contempt goes along with it, together with the super-sensitivity to opinions, to the approval, and the disapproval of others. And all of this is accompanied by a cloud of guilt.

The perfectionist almost has to feel guilty - if for nothing else, for not feeling guilty about something! Perfectionism produces a distorted picture...There is a cure for perfectionism....to experience the cure you need to accept the prescription for the process of healing.[39]

Again, you are the safety net for the narcissist. Thus, you become their adviser. However, they think they are smarter and superior to you. They trivialize everything you say. They recuse themselves of any guilt for wrongdoing and you soak it in. You are the problem solver. You are their problem and the solution, "If you would just." This makes them tune you out and dismissive to what you say to them. This also makes you tune out the disrespect, pain, word salad and injustice made legal. Why? Because you are a people-pleaser. You want acceptance. You tolerate injurious behavior to keep things

---

39 Seamands. David A. *Healing for Damaged Emotions*. Life Journey-Cook Communication Ministries printing. Colorado Springs, CO. 2004.

going with the appearance of being copasetic. You are self-sacrificing to the point it pains you to not put someone else's needs first above your very own.

The more it does not work, the harder you try to make it work and get better. You are a yes man/woman, always willing to help out and go the extra mile and be there for someone who has demonstrated that you are there for their needs, but you seldom, if ever, can count on them. They triangulate you with their ex and their next and you have now come to realize that you are a collector's item to them. That is who you are in part.

You are loveable and capable of being loved properly. You are strong and full of love and joy. You are interesting enough. You are intelligent enough. You are probably overqualified for them. But do not hate yourself for being willing to compromise your standards to make others happy. One day, you will move from helping others to helping yourself. You will move from crossing oceans for others to crossing your legs and relaxing.

You will move from being manipulated to becoming completely unbothered by their childish tactics. You will move from ungrateful to grateful to know and have met you. You are a dream come true to someone. You are the answer to someone's prayer. You are what the doctor ordered. You are the solution to the problem. Unfortunately, it is not with the narcissist. You may have wanted the relationship to work out, but they did not. That narcissist was probably your greatest lesson and blessing. You are stronger now because you woke up. You are aware of the games and tricks. You are smart. You are intelligent. You are recovering from complex post-traumatic stress disorder dealing with a person with narcissistic personality disorder. It will take time to heal. But you have got this.

You are not under the spell anymore. You woke up from the beautiful nightmare and discovered that wolf in sheep's clothing. You saw the mask slip and now, you cannot unsee it. You heard the delusions and knew that they cannot follow through with anything because they do not have the capacity to do so.

You are amazing. Yes, for love, or what you thought was love, you let someone walk all over you. Yes, you compromised but you also compromised your self-esteem and let another person establish your self-worth. Knowing this, you do not need them. They need you. In fact, they need you way more than you ever needed them. You may want them, but you do not need them. Pets do not need fleas, ticks, and worms. In the same manner, you do not need the narcissist. You care too much about what they think. But do not hate yourself for caring.

This world needs people who care. One thing is for sure; two things are certain. You are not and will never have to choose to be an option. If you find yourself with a narcissist and they are straddling the fence with you as an option, help that clown out and make the choice for them and tell them to choose the other person. Why? You are not a damn option. You are the choice. If they cannot get with it, leave that person to go be with who they think will make them happy. They are already thinking they can do better without you. Make them stand on that. I promise you, there is someone out there who will love, respect, listen, validate, appreciate, and participate in life <u>with</u> you. You just have to let the trash take itself out. You are a good soul. Now be good or be good at it.

I'd rather my silence be misunderstood than my words be misquoted, or my presence mishandled.
~Morgan Richard Oliver

I forgive myself for viewing someone's lack of reciprocation as a challenge to convince them of my worth.

~ Unknown

"*When someone says to you, 'I don't deserve you.' You better start believing them because they are about to show you.*"
~*Sandy Tencer*

CHAPTER 18

APOLOGIES FROM NARCISSISTS AND WHAT THEY REALLY MEAN.

Narcissists do not apologize truly. They do not apologize because they think they are right all the time, so why apologize when they were right and justified in their action? In the movie 'Get Rich or Die Tryin,' Terrence Howard's character, Bama says, to Curtus "50 Cent" Jackson's character Markus, "…I'm always right. It is like when I'm right, I'm right. And when I'm wrong, I could have been right. So, I'm still right because I could have been wrong." Do not ever ask for or expect an apology from a narcissist. They said what they meant and meant what they said. Angry or not, they meant it when they said and did it.

That is how they feel, and an apology only means they were wrong. The narcissist may also never apologize because they think time will make you forget it (things). If you do not bring it up, then it's out of sight, out of mind. Perhaps by ignoring it, it means it did not happen. Since the narcissist lacks empathy or accountability, they ultimately think it is your fault, so they will not offer an apology. Because the narcissist is so entitled, they do not think you deserve a genuine apology. They may also have every intention of doing whatever they did again. The lies they tell suit them and not the person being lied to. Their apologies are disingenuous and faux apologies. They may apologize by saying something along the lines of,

"I'm sorry if I hurt you."

"I'm sorry for making things hard for you."

"I'm sorry I cheated."

"I'm sorry I can't be the man/woman you deserve."

Translations – I am sorry you are so sensitive; I wish you would toughen up. I am upset that you could not be blind while I keep the façade up and keep me financially supplied without detecting that I do not want to do anything but leech off your success. I am upset that you figured out I was cheating because I was having fun disrespecting you and being sneaky. I am not going to change so take it or leave it.

These are not apologies. But here are a few additional things that narcissists may also say,

◊ "I am sorry, okay, happy now? Sheesh. You are so sensitive."

◊ "You are making this a bigger deal than it is."

◊ "Relax; you are being a stick in the mud."

◊ "Why aren't you laughing? You act like you have a stick up your butt."

◊ "I am sorry, but you have done stuff too. What about when you…" [Leveling]

◊ "My intention was not to hurt you." [Because you were never supposed to find out]

◊ "I was only joking - you know that, right?"

◊ "I will apologize if you also apologize for…."

◊ "I'm sorry for how it made you feel, but I meant what I said."

◊ "I am sorry you cannot take my jokes. Lighten up a little."

◊ "I regret what happened, but it's kind of your fault."

◊ "If you had been here, I never would have cheated."

◊ "I've done wrong, but you have done things too."

◊ "I'll apologize but you have to promise to never bring it up again."

Other quotes and translations may include;

◊ **"Your too sensitive"** I just said something cruel, mean, and heartless, and I want to make your reaction the problem to my comments so I can play victim.

◊ **"Let's just focus on the good"** – Ignore all my red flags, gaslighting and manipulations.

◊ **"You're overreacting"** – Your emotional response threatens my control of you and I want to minimize your responses.

◊ **"You are so selfish"** – You are standing up for yourself and not being my puppet and that makes me angry because I cannot control you easily anymore.

◊ **"I never said that"** – I absolutely said that but now I'm gaslighting you to confuse the way you remember things.

◊ **"I guess I can't do anything right"** – I'm faking sympathy for the outcome of what decision I made, and I want you to have pity on me so I can escape accountability.

◊ **"Don't blame me, You made me do this"** – I refuse to take accountability and twisting this on you makes me feel better.

◊ **"Everyone agrees with me"** – I'm lying and or I want you to feel isolated and outnumbered so you stop talking about it.

◊ **"You win"** – I am in secret competition with you and I cannot outthink or manipulate you so I am faking surrender so I can regroup and find leverage for later.

◊ **"I guess I'm just the worst person ever"** – I'll fake self-pity and not hold myself accountable and you'll come to my rescue and focus on pitying me instead of

◊ **"You deserve better than me"** – I am appearing to devaluing myself to devalue you into rescuing me with gratefulness for having me in your life. This phrase from the narcissist plays on insecurities and fosters a push-pull dynamic where the narcissist simultaneously devalues themselves to the empath all while implying their partner should be grateful.

◊ **"Why can't you just let go of the past?"** – I do not want to deal with how I hurt you, I want you to forget what happened and let it go so I do not feel shame.

◊ **"You're just jealous and being insecure"** – I am definitely triangulating you with someone who I may have had dealings with.

◊ **"You're crazy"** – you see through me and that scares me.

◊ **"You'll never find someone like me"** – I'm trying to scare you into staying with me, even though I know I have mistreated you when you didn't leave.

◊ **"I love you"** – I love how much you tolerate, and let me use you and have my way without resistance as a yes man, but do I respect you, NO.

◊ **"You did this to yourself"** – I am recusing myself of any responsibility so blame yourself.

◊ **"Well, are you going to break up with me or what?"** **[after getting caught with proof of infidelity]** – I am regretting that you caught on to my superior self and I do not want to explain. As a matter of fact, I am going to keep doing it. So do you want to stay or not?

Reader, the truth is, the best apology is changed behavior. There is a difference between repentance and an apology. When a person or people are Godly sorry, it leads to repentance. Repentance is turning from evil and pejorative ways. It is the consequence of a character shift, which the narcissist lacks. The objective in true repentance is the effort to make things right, set the record straight, and then even become indignant with one's own heart for offending and not being angry at the offended for feeling offended by the behavior. Repentance is about acknowledging that one misrepresented the character of God, which is truth, love and faithfulness. Moreover, repentance is way more than simply saying, "I did that." and "I'm sorry." When practiced properly, there is an obvious transformation exemplified by character shift that shows authenticity.

Because the narcissists are stuck in a certain phase or stage of life, they are likely incapable of change. They are programmed to get their own way and do not care who it is in front of them or in their circle; they will use them to advance their cause. They would rather leave you than change. They would rather do all the things you want for someone else than give them to you, because they have devalued you in their mind and deemed you undeserving of the things you require. They are going to push you to discard or reverse discard them before it is all over.

At best, they will offer you a faux apology mixed with future faking and empty promise making. They will promise you the world, then ask you to fund them giving you the world. Then reverse that and tell you that you owe them the world. It should be what you are doing for them. They may cry with tears in their eyes and fall to the floor begging you to forgive them and yet still not change. They may fall down like a toddler does in a grocery store when they want something

DR. BYRAM MCKINZIE, SR.

on a certain aisle, but know that it is all an act. It is rehearsed and scripted. They will do the very thing they promised not to do again. Next time they are just going to be sneakier with it.

If you cause a narcissist a narcissistic injury, they will never forgive you. In the recesses of their mind, they are conjuring up a plan to get revenge. They will likely not forgive you. The rationale behind not forgiving you is that they get to hold you hostage in their mind. As a prisoner of war in their mind, they will torture you every chance they get.

Forgiving you would free you and they would have to take responsibility or some form of accountability. Their ego cannot accept that they are to blame for any of what did or did not happen. Facing responsibility and forgiving people are really two sides of the same coin. The reason some people have never been able to forgive is that if they forgave, the last rug would be pulled out from under them, and they would have no one to blame. Facing responsibility and forgiving are almost the same action; in some instances, you need to do them simultaneously.[40]

If the narcissist/psychopath was honest, this is what he or she should say aloud to you: "I only pay you compliments to lower your guard. I need time. Time to fill your head with all the things you want to hear. I will never love you truly, but I will fake it and act like I do to get what I want from you. I am a coward, a fraud and a fake. I do this because I know I can get away with it and you will either give me another chance or

---

40   David A. Seamands. *Healing for Damaged Emotions.* Life Journey-Cook Communication Ministries printing. Colorado Springs, CO. 2004.

leave me. Deep down inside, you know I am wrong, but the words I say to you & my act are so good that you ignore your intuition, even when I let the mask slip. Now I have you right where I need you to be....ignoring what you know is best for you and always making excuses for me. I am sorry that I am not sorry. But you chose me. You now know what it is now. Take it or leave it. But if you stay, do not complain, or bring it up because I am going to do it again and I do not want to feel the shame of knowing I am not as amazing as I present myself to be." This behavior is stonewalling.

The design is to keep them from taking any accountability or responsibility, and deflecting and shifting the blame. Trust the pattern and not their words of inconsistency. The message they say is what they say and want to be. The patters and pathology do not lie. Behavior repeats like a cycle of winter, spring, summer, and fall. The message can shift the moment, but behavior repeats. If you were paying attention, the truth/facts were never hidden. You saw and heard what you wanted until you saw and heard what you needed to see.

A real apology is remorse followed by silence, space & changed behavior. A real apology is less speaking and more personal work on yourself. A real apology is looking within and addressing what causes you to hurt someone you love.
~Limitless Mind

CHAPTER 19

HOW TO HEAL FROM NARCISSISTIC ABUSE

When finding your voice in the room:

1. Feel your emotions. (Let them pass, but feel them.)
2. Get a licensed professional therapist to help you facilitate your process. You probably have C-PTSD. You need professional help.
3. Speak up for yourself.
4. Listen to the thinking voice in your head. Some call it their gut, or intuition or vibes. The voice in your head can talk and talk and talk. It never needs to take a breath. It does not get out of breath. Silence can help you find your voice.
5. Go Gray Rock. Become lukewarm to all their games.
6. Process the trauma (get therapy if needed).
7. Educate yourself about what happened.
8. Redefine yourself. Self-discovery is about discovering who you are versus who you think you are.

9. Remember - the whole thing was a fake, a façade, a camouflage suit. You were in a relationship with a mirror image of yourself and the mask slipped.

10. Tell your story. You saved their reputation by not telling your side of the story. When asked, tell your side of the story.

11. Find your tribe. Finding your tribe is a journey of self-discovery and connection with people who have been through or are experiencing similar things.

We should not trust a narcissist for several distinct reasons. We should never trust someone who we know will hurt and betray us. If you assume you should trust everyone, then you can be taken advantage of in the worst way, especially by a narcissist or a toxic personality. Narcissists can be likeable, and we believe likeable people are trustworthy, which is not always the truth. Their behavior can cause you to let your guard down and when you do, they will pull a fast one on you.

They do not play fair and will throw a curveball your way when you least expect it. Sometimes our brain is not even able to catch up with their manipulation. They feed off depression, low esteem, loyalty, naivety, kindness, and good nature. They really want to know what really hurts you so they can use that against you in every conceivable way. You will always be the one trying to adjust to what they want or need. You will feel drained and tired after being around them due to their negativity. You will feel exhausted, fatigued, drained, off balance, on edge, and loaded with anxiety all the time. You will always feel like you are on a battlefield when dealing with them. You are literally dealing with psychological warfare when dealing with someone who has NPD - narcissistic personality disorder. They will destroy your self-esteem, confidence, self-worth, and ability to trust others. They are predatory abusers, and users only look out to feed their sick, twisted depravity of intentionally abusing, using, misleading, and manipulating others.

You should never trust them, because they will keep you guessing about which version of them you are getting. Narcissists figured out a long time ago that decent, good people like you will go to extraordinary lengths to keep them happy, content, and comfortable. Narcissists have a way of making you feel as if you owe them something or that you are responsible for their happiness.

They also have a way of taking from you without giving anything in return. They will pour salt on your wounds to hurt you even more, especially if they know your vulnerabilities, weakness, or deep secrets. Narcissists love to humiliate or manipulate others, particularly when they are most vulnerable. Do not give them any ammunition and be very mindful about what you reveal or share with them.

The more you share or do for them, the more you are at risk to be weaponized by them in the worst way imaginable. They are dangerous, selfish, emotionally stunted, and mentally exhausting, which is why we should **never** trust a narcissist. May you know the signs, may you not be a victim, and may you do whatever you need to do to protect your emotional-mental health.[41]

Beloved, if you continue to betray yourself because you do not listen to your body signal that something is not right, the universe has this unique way of bringing someone into your external proximity who will betray you so badly because you were not able to say no yourself.

Please know. that those who do not express their boundaries clearly or speak their truth with conviction but carry on suppressing and suppressing and suppressing have the highest rate of cancers. Mostly all diseases that have to be made manifest somehow reveal themselves because you have been suppressing your truth and feelings for so long that your body is simply trying to heal itself from things that cannot get out of it fast enough.

Your body is an instrument of consciousness. When there is mental conflict, it says to us, "There some dissonance." Your body is magically telling you that there is something misaligned. The behavior, the boundary crossing, the Freudian slips, gaslighting, dog-whistling, and other silent killers are all things that go against your peace and well-being. When you recognize this, speak the truth with conviction. Even if they do not want to hear it.

You absolutely must choose yourself this time. No more excuses.
Remain committed to success. Stay loyal to your dreams.
~Lewis Showes

---

41   https://www.quora.com/Why-should-we-not-trust-a-narcissist Taken 12/12/2023.

CHAPTER 20

BREAKING THE SPELL

In order to get out and ever live a peaceful life, there must be a turning point. A time of awakening, if you will. Once that happens, there is no going back. Now, I do not mean that you may never get back together with the narcissist; that happens all the time. When I say there is no going back, I mean that things will no longer be the same, at least not mentally. Once you see a situation for what it is, there is a sense of clarity that comes with it and things are no longer what they appear. It is as if the veil has been lifted and you now understand things in a much clearer light. With that light may come some shock, sadness, and discomfort. You are now seeing the person you love for what they truly are and that this is not a normal happy relationship. - Jade Asikiwe.[42]

---

42 Asikiwe, Jade. *Overcoming Narcissistic Relationships as an Empath: Breaking the Karmic Cycles of Empaths and Narcissists.* Coppell, TX.

I have a saying, "Sometimes it ain't what it is. It is what it looks like." If it walks like a duck and talks like a duck. Come on!! It is a duck. It looks like you were a fool. It looks like you were getting played. It looked like you were defeated. It looked like you were silenced. It looked like you were TKO'ed.

However, do not make the mistake of hating yourself for being a loving and caring individual. Be grateful that you caught on to the fact that the manipulation and games were being played on you and that you realized it for yourself. Unlove them, because the person you love does not exist. The person you love or think you love is an imposter. They are a relationship chameleon. They do not love you genuinely.

Their loyalty is only for the need of you. Once the need for your resources changed, didn't they? When they got the better job, did they not abandon you? They got a new ride; did you not see their lover in it? You discovered they had two phones. Did you not find out that there were multiple pseudonyms of people they had and were planning to see? When they found the new supply, did they not sneak around and cheat, lie, omit, abandon, disrespect, and stonewall you? Did they not steal your identity and use it to advance themselves without your prior consent? Did they not accuse you of the very thing they were doing? Wake up!

Ending a relationship with a narcissist is anything but easy. It can be as mentally and emotionally exhausting as dealing with them on a day-to-day basis. You would think by saying, 'it's over' they would get the message and move on. Not so with these people. Narcissist hate losing their supply, especially on short notice. They do not go gently into the night, especially if they are not done with you.[43]

To break the spell, you have to become indifferent to their games. The opposite of love is not hate. It is indifference. At least with hate, there is energy and effort to not like you, but with indifference, there is no care at all. Your goal should be no touch, no talk, no eye contact, no communication at all. Do not text, email, snail mail or any form of communication if it is possible. These are the things you must do to get over the make-believe relationship. You may have to practice what Mark Manson suggests in his book, *The Subtle art of not giving a f*ck,* and that is not giving a f*ck.

Quit giving a damn about anything they say or do which is disrespectful and takes away your peace. They are trying to provoke a response from you to get supply. Become done. Not reactive. Not upset. Just done. No looking on their social media to get updates on what they are doing with the new supply. Ninety percent of social media posts are nothing more than moments of happiness and grandstanding. Anybody can post the appearance of moments of happiness. Them posting is nothing more than attempts to get external validation, which again is another form of supply.

---

43 Louise, Rita, PhD. *The Dysfunctional Dance of the Empath and the Narcissist: Create Healthy Relationships by Healing Childhood Trauma.* Library of Congress. First Edition. Dallas, TX.

The dopamine rush they used to give has ended. You no longer get high and lows of the emotional rollercoaster they had you on. That hamster wheel of going nowhere but demonstrating motion to you is clear now. They lost their charm.

They no longer have that 'je ne sais quoi'. That narcissist's ego caused them to breadcrumb and devalue you, and that is when they messed up. While the frequency was high, they were under the radar. Too much mask slipping and breadcrumbing mixed with disrespect, passive aggressive behavior, and the need to be right exposed them. Game. Set. Match.

You were never supposed to figure it out. You were never supposed to figure out the game that was being played on you. You were never supposed to figure out, on your own, any of the things listed in this book about their behavior. You were never supposed to discover they were a relationship chameleon. You were never supposed to notice their patterns. You were never supposed to discover they were **future faking** to buy themselves some time to keep the façade going. You were never supposed to figure out how to cut the cord, sever the ties, detach, run away, mirror the narcissist, and get away from their dysfunctional behavior.

You were supposed to stay blind and be a good supply. You were supposed to have unwavering empathy for them. You were supposed to stay under the puppet master's manipulative control of the temper tantrum throwing child trapped in the adult's body. But a still small voice inside you kept telling you, "Something is not right." "This is not love." "Nobody that loves me would actually treat me this way." "Nobody that loves me could disrespect me intentionally." "No one that loves me would talk, plan, meet, set up, and execute an affair and come home like nothing ever happened." "I should not keep discovering new things that they have done that I knew nothing about."

That is not love. Love mixed with respect would never do that. True love would have them just break it off with you before they cheat or disrespect you EVER. The disrespect is a reflection of how they feel about you and your worth to the relationship. Snap out of it! They do not love you. They never did.

Whether you know this or not, the narcissist gaslit you so much in that relationship that you are probably **self-gaslighting** yourself now. You probably were blaming yourself for why they cannot get their act together. The narcissist made a crucial mistake when they let that mask slip and started getting comfortable misbehaving with you. Their arrogance and pride brought them to the ruin of the relationship. It is a good thing, but do not underestimate your silent opponent.

To know your greatest weakness is to know your strength. To know your greatest strength is also knowing an area of weakness. A good strategist takes away someone's perceived strengths and make them win another way. You may know them well. You may think you have them all figured out. However, the best way to deal with a narcissist is to not. They are skilled at turning things around on you. As the adult in the parent-child relationship you will find yourself sympathizing and empathizing with them. Coddling and bailing them out of bad situations that cost you your peace. They are skilled at turning their crisis into your emergency. Let them catch that negative karma or else you will catch it by staying with them.

They cast a strong spell. However, it is time to break the spell. This book is the start of your spell breaker. The actual spell they cast on you was nothing more than words [love bombing, idealization, word salad, emotional gymnastics, and future faking with a well-dressed package of lies] and actions [sex bombing, rage, physical abuse, abandoning, silent treatment].

They cloned and mirrored you. It is like putting someone under hypnosis and telling them what you want them to do and watching them do it. It is like playing a jedi mind trick, but you caught on. Words that used to be in the following form: guilt trips, insults, shame, and the need to be right shaped your thoughts with them. Now you are cognizant of what they did, and you can counter all their words and actions which are designed to get a reaction out of you. You have become aware of your feelings and how your body reacts when you are in their presence, listening to their words. You are not stuck in **cognitive dissonance** anymore because you know what they were trying to do.

But today, you realize you have had an awakening. You are constantly coming from under their spell. Their words do not matter like they used to. Their words do not carry weight because you already know they are empty promises of **future faking** mixed with **breadcrumbing** to keep you hopeful.

You understand they are pathological liars who will be in the same space years from now. You understand they are an aging narcissist whose supply options and pickings are getting low. Thus, they are just desperately attempting to secure their uncertain future. You understand that they are a serial cheater and that reflects their character, and not a lack of your ability in the relationship you share with them.

That mask slipped and you saw them through their façade. You recognize the camouflage suit hidden in plain sight. You have become numb to the games. You now know the slick remarks are nothing but **dog whistling.** You now know you are powerful, otherwise they would not have to get people on their side to convince them about how lacking you are. You have understood something clearly at last and cannot unsee it. You have probably learned to love yourself and put you first. Regardless of what anyone says, loving yourself is a superpower.

Loving yourself does not mean you are selfish. It means you treat yourself with respect. It means you can be nice but do not accept nor tolerate disrespect as a mistaken behavior masquerading as trying to love you. It means you speak nicely to yourself. It means you affirm you, even if no one else does. It means you find peace within and grow it like a tree. The narcissist is committed to chaos.

You are committed to peace. Loving yourself means accepting you are who you are and what you are. You now see that counterproductive behavior is not love. Anyone not wanting to see you grow and glow obviously does not love you.

Love is not envious. You found out and now you are aware. You are cognizant of the facts now. That makes you informed and powerful. They cannot hustle you into advancing their cause while they **goldbrick** you.

You have seen plainly how they will abandon you, leave you neglected all while going to the ends of the earth for someone else in their time of need. You clearly recognize they will go over an ocean for someone else but have obvious issues with going over a puddle for you. You woke up from that beautiful nightmare and realized that all the stuff they talked about was made of dreams.

The walls, money, love, car, house, grass, people, jobs, vacations were all made of dreams. The reality is they will never change under any circumstances. They will only adapt and keep on pretending. Now you have noticed the pattern and know for sure they are predictable. Please understand, if they are having to collect teammates or flying monkeys to go up against you, you must be powerful all by yourself. That is how powerful you are!

If you are thinking of going back to them, let me place an ancient text before you. Matthew 12:43-45: "When an **unpure spirit** comes out of a person, it goes through arid places seeking rest and does not find it. Then it says, 'I will return to the house I left.'" When it arrives, it finds the house unoccupied, swept clean and put in order.

Then it goes and takes with it seven other spirits more wicked than itself, and they go in and live there. The final condition of that person is worse than the first.

We cannot change what we are not aware of, and once we are aware, we cannot help but to change.

~Sheryl Sandberg

CHAPTER 21

THE FINAL DISCARD OF THE NARCISSIST

The steps of narcissistic abuse are: One Love bombing/ Idealization → Two. Devaluation → Three. Discard → Four. Hoovering, and Five. Repetition. When dealing with the discard phase, it can happen multiple ways. The very things they seemed to love and dote on you for are the very things they hate and envy you for. If you are intelligent, they love it in the beginning but hate that you are intelligent enough to figure them out. If they love your looks, they will hate that you are either handsome or beautiful as you may draw away attention from them.

This is likely the devaluation phase where nothing that once was good enough matters anymore. When they are discarding you, they have already secured the next supply [monkey branching] and are now ready for the relationship to end with you. They can discard you as a woman does a used menstrual pad or they can treat you so badly that they cause you to want out of the relationship. This tactic is known as the reverse discard. Again, the relationship started with idealization, love bombing and maybe even sex bombing. But later, after they get bored and find a new more suitable supply to replace you, they have to discard you to run the game on the next person.

Discard or reverse discard is the third and often closing phase of the abuse people feel from narcissists. This phase often leaves the partner feeling worthless and confused and wondering what they could have done differently to salvage the relationship. The narcissist was always planning to leave.

The narcissist was always measuring up when would be enough money, time, disrespect, disregard and disdain to leave you for. In reality, no amount of effort would have changed the relationship's outcome, as the narcissist is always looking for new victims to pad their ego.[44] This discard phase can be confusing because they may function as if they do not want you, while also attempting to make sure no one else has you. Remember, some narcissists see you as a possession.

This is the hoovering that the narcissist does. They pop up at work. They go to your parents' or family's house to see you. They monitor your social media to get updates on your information. They may pop up at places they know you frequently attend to spy or have their flying monkeys

---

44 The Narcissistic Life. The Narcissist Discard Phase: 3 Signs A final Discard is Coming. https://thenarcissisticlife.com/narcissist-discard/

report back to them. However, none of this matters, as you are expendable and replaceable.

The discard can be subtle or bitter, but is likely never to be amicable with a narcissist. They do not want you anymore in the discard phase because you are not Grade A supply anymore. They want the supply without restrictions. But they also do not want anyone else to have you, as it may work out well with the other person. They no longer see you as positive supply. They see you as negative supply. Either way, as long as they are in some sort of relationship with you [close or distant], there is some supply.

They start doing things that will annoy you so that the decision to end the relationship comes from you. Their motives are clear if you understand the patterns of discard. There may be many goals in mind, but three main ones are often employed. The first is getting as much usable supply from you as they possibly can, while giving little-to-nothing in the form of reciprocation. They do not have the wherewithal to make it without a supply or group of suppliers. They never have and never will.

So, it is essential that they store up what they can get from you and others. A little here and a little there adds up. The second is leaving you in the worst way imaginable to crush you. They may leave you while you are at work. They may drain the bank accounts and ghost you. They may take all the equity out of the house and leave you with the mortgage. They may engage in white-collar crimes like running lines of credit up in your name and leaving you to foot the bill.

They may start a business and let it go bankrupt. The third thing is leaving with enough plausible deniability that they still look like saints or victims in the story. They are almost always guaranteed to make themselves look like the victim or hero in the story.

To create this illusion of plausible deniability takes work. They must know how long they have to stay married to you in order to get alimony estate. They calculate how much child support each child can yield them. They buy shares in stock or invest in business with you for long-term supply. They do this because they are thinking they have to keep you invested long enough that you put them through school, or you put them back on their feet.

Also, you probably have a clean reputation, so next they have to gauge public perception to know when to leave you if you get terminally ill. Why? Because you were supposed to take care of them, and not have them taking care of you without a return on their investment. You soon discover they execute matters with such callous disregard for your feelings that it changes your whole outlook on life.

Not everyone who engages in ghosting behavior is necessarily a narcissist. However, ghosting is a typical behavior of the narcissist as they are attempting to discard. If you suffer from separation anxiety, you may become emotionally exhausted when the narcissist uses threats of leaving to manipulate you. They may start to look for someone new since the narcissist requires constant praise and ego boosting. They do not care for the correction. The new supply is giving them the praise they seek. The new supply does not know they are a relationship chameleon. Next, you may notice that the affection they used to give comes to a screeching halt. The making of time for you to stay connected stops. The hugs stop. The sex and intimacy slow to almost none and then stop. The preparing of meals stops. The attempts to nourish you stop.

The supporting of your aspirations stops. The effort stops. They simply stop trying. The distance increases. The "I love you's" stop. They may lie and blame it on them being tired. But notice that they are too tired for you, but they make time and have enough energy to do stuff for someone else and insult you by letting you know they are going to do it for them. Next, they pick a fight with you and blame you for the relationship's failure.

Often, the narcissist will pick fights when you are stuck in a moving vehicle with them. The narcissist may use the vehicle as a dungeon of torture because you are on the road and are bound to the vehicle for the duration of the drive. That vehicle is a tank with the weapons of mass destruction coming out of the mouth of the narcissist. Any mistake you make while driving, they will enumerate thus frustrating you because concentration on the road is a top priority.

They keep talking and belittling and criticizing and griping and complaining and making life hell. They may say, "I can't do this anymore." The discard phase could be quick. However, if you have been in relationship with them a long time, it could be a long, drawn-out process where you are made to feel undeserving, worthless, spiritually constipated and emotionally exhausted for things not working out. The ultimate move of the narcissist is to destroy you or get you to your lowest form. When the narcissist finally leaves, whether by moving out or divorcing you, it is only because they are in a better position to leave you with almost nothing. Notice the silent treatment.

Notice how they are gone longer and longer. Notice how they ask you less and less. Notice how they gather the troops against you. The final coup-de-grâce is when they try to get you to see yourself as unloved and unlovable. They know that you love deeply and sincerely. By discarding you, in their mind they think it will crush you and cause you to want to just crawl under a rock and die. They may start giving you the silent treatment.

The male narcissist is excellent in doing this as men tend to retreat within and process inwardly when things are bothering them. Female narcissists who are silent know that it is over, and they tend to use silence to keep you guessing what you did wrong or could have done to fix it.

The reverse discard may include behaviors like cheating where you can find it. It may also include bringing you to financial ruin. They will break boundaries and push your limits until you break it off with them. This allows them to be the victim in the story they concocted. If they are the victim in the story, you'd better believe you will become the villain in that same story. Be the villain if it means you will be free of that energy vampire. They know what they are doing.

That relationship chameleon is impulsive, needy, has short attention spans, poor emotional regulations, hypersensitivity, lacks empathy, lacks accountability, has relentless unrealistic expectations, cannot take any constructive criticism of any kind without suffering narcissistic injury, and has a superiority complex and suffers from narcissistic collapse when they do not get their delusional ways.

They probably demanded you get rid of your ex or certain friends, but they keep their former lovers, one-night stands, and lie telling you they are just friends. When confronted, they do all they can to keep that person. But notice that they blocked them but did not unfriend them. They also did not put them in their place in a way that you heard them do it.

They never told them, "It's over; we can't do this anymore," in front of you. Why? For future reference/supply, that narcissist will unblock them and communicate with them when you are so-called taking a break or in some down time. And this is what you have been putting up with. Triangulation.

You walked on eggshells. Did that help you? No; they still managed to discard you. You stayed faithful. You served their needs even when there was no return other than you being satisfied with doing for them. They still managed to blame you for the failure of the marriage, the children's growing pains, the financial lack, and why they cannot get their sh*t together. Next in the discard and reverse discard phase, you are likely to experience them practicing a form of indifference or duality. They will let you be the one to break it off. This inaction was allowed for future references; they can remind you that you ended the relationship. It leaves the door open for a return. However, they may get another person and tell you to go on with your life.

The possible final move is hoovering. Narcissistic hoovering refers to intentional behavior made by the narcissist to bring their victim back into their life. Hoovering may begin at any time after the devaluation or discard phase. The narcissist may feel that there is distance being made by the victim and they have to try to reel the victim back into them - like a yo-yo master flicks their wrist and watches you come rolling back to them with the string attached. The methods could include emailing, texting, inboxing, DM-ing, calling, withdrawing signed divorce papers just before the ninety days, showing up at places you are very likely to appear, posting and tagging you on social media, or snail mailing.

The likelihood is that the narcissist will employ this tactic when they fear the supply is moving away emotionally or possibly has gained personal empowerment. The very term hoovering is reminiscent of a vacuum; thus, the narcissist will vacuum up your happiness, positivity, hope, optimism as supply for them. Do not fall for it. Them coming back is just to finish you off. They spun the block, saw there was no more stabler grade A supply and circled back. They will return to try to give you the death blow. Let it and them go. No touch. No talk. No contact. You will get over them.

The deliverance and freedom that comes with realizing and accepting that people can only love at the capacity with which they love themselves, and/or treat others at the capacity with which they treat themselves, destroys the self-inflicted torment of feeling "less than" or "not good enough" based on how someone else loves or treats you.

Free yourself and Be FREE!!!

~ Claudia A. Steele

*The moment anyone tries to demean or degrade you in any way,
you have to know how great you are. Nobody would bother to
beat you down if you were not a threat.*

~ Cicely Tyson

CHAPTER 22

FINDING YOUR VOICE IN THE ROOM

"When you get up on this podium, I want you to look out in that audience and I want you to think to yourself **"I'm a voice in this world damnit, and I deserve to be heard."**

Finding your voice in the room requires you knowing the strength you have in your own words. You will never hear another person's voice more than you hear your own. Be intentional about the way that you talk to yourself. You must speak the truth. Your truth. In your lifetime you talked yourself into some things and you will also talk yourself out of some things. Many things you said "yes" to. However, you found it difficult to say no to people because you wanted acceptance and are accommodating.

Finding your voice in a room begins with self-awareness and confidence. Understand your values, beliefs, and the unique perspectives you bring to the table. Prepare yourself by thinking about the key points you want to convey and the reasons behind them.

When you enter the room, take a moment to observe the dynamics and identify the right opportunity to speak up. Make sure to listen actively to others; this shows respect and helps you gauge the conversation, allowing you to contribute thoughtfully and relevantly.

Proverbs 18: 21 says, 'Life and death are in the power of the tongue: and they that love it shall eat the fruit thereof.' We all want to feel heard when we express our wants, needs, and desires. Knowing we have been heard allows us to feel connected to the other person and as if we matter in their life. When two people can communicate openly and freely, it leads to better outcomes in the relationship and issues can be resolved quicker.[45]

When using your voice, speak clearly and assertively, ensuring your words are heard and understood. Use a calm and composed demeanor to convey your message effectively. Avoid being confrontational; instead, aim for constructive dialogue, presenting your ideas with confidence and backing them up with evidence when needed. Remember to maintain eye contact and use body language that demonstrates your engagement and conviction. Standing or sitting upright, leaning slightly forward, and using hand gestures can emphasize your points and show your enthusiasm.

45   Emily Mayfield. *Why are problems never solved with Narcissists?* https://www.mindsettherapyonline.com

Narcissists have methods and tactics they use when they're arguing with you and being disagreeable. Here are four different techniques narcissists use when arguing with you.

◊ 1. **Interrupting** – Narcissists are masters at interrupting you while you are talking. To avoid accountability they will always interrupt you when you are speaking, often never letting you share your side of the story, point of view or concerns. Whenever you try to communicate, they will just shut you down, stonewalling you, raising their voice, overtalking you, and interrupting every single sentence so you can never fully express yourself. That will cause you severe frustration. In doing this the argument goes around in circles making it feel never-ending. Thus, there is no resolution. Only diversion from one topic to another topic. The conflict either gets forgotten or continues endlessly until you are so exhausted that you drop it.

◊ 2. **Intimidating behavior** – narcissists will use intimidating behavior such as bullying, threatening, raging, yelling, gesturing, and fearmongering to silence you. The narcissist may raise their voice, getting louder and louder until you retreat. You being an empath wants everyone to have a chance to speak. They might also physically intimidate you by getting closer, making you fearful and threatening you so that you stop speaking altogether. This causes you to minimize everything you need to say for fear of their reaction.

◇ 3. **Minimizing your feelings** – the narcissist will minimize your feelings and thoughts; making fun of you, putting you down, criticizing and complaining that your emotions are ridiculous, and your thought process is crazy. They make you feel like you are the perpetrator, and they are the reasonable one.

◇ 4. **Projection** – they will project their own issues onto you, making you feel like you are the one causing the problem. The narcissist has a unique way of insisting on getting their way because, in their mind, their way is better and you do not have the knowledge of how to speak on some subjects. Therefore, you are the problem because you will not comply with their ideal solution.

Armed with this information, understand that there is a much bigger game being played on you than you likely can imagine. You are their emotional regulator. In a sinister manner, they need you to either bow down or rage. Either way, they get a supply. They are attempting to classically condition you to accept their toxic behavior as the norm so they can avoid accountability and responsibility.

Through the conditioning process over a duration of time, you make the observation and correlation that every time you do XYZ, it makes them angry. In most cases the XYZ equates to you calling them out for their behavior. It could also be that XYZ is you attempting to hold them accountable for something because they have made you feel like they are angry - it is your fault and you bringing it up is the problem. After all, you have the problem and the solution. However, since you want to get along, you have learned over time not to bring these things up as this way, you can prevent them from getting angry. Every time you do this, you betray yourself by not living in your truth.

In another light, you are slowly learning that even if you react it will not change anything. Reacting will not make some people suddenly love and respect you. It will not magically change their minds about you. Sometimes it is better to just let things be. Let people go. Do not fight for closure. Do not ask for explanations. What is understood does not need to be explained. Do not chase answers and do not expect people to understand where you are coming from when you try to explain. You are slowly learning that life is better lived when you do not center it on what is happening around you, but rather center it on what is happening within. Work on yourself and your inner peace.

Learning to say "NO" and not explain is a superpower. Learning to say "Yes" to yourself and your needs is also a superpower. This can be challenging while dealing with a narcissist because you put the needs of others above yours, they are never wrong, and they do not like taking no for an answer. You are used to being a yes man. But now you have a set of boundaries for yourself. You are saying no to:

1. Them getting back with you because together you are toxic

2. Their future-faking grandiose ideas since you now know it is a scheme to buy time

3. Being their fiduciary [for their childish plan] because you know they are irresponsible with their finances

4. Being their punching bag, verbally or physically

5. Their toxic subtle or overt disrespect

When finding your voice, remember you are an original. One of one. Nobody is better at being you than you, even though that narcissist tried to clone you. Your words do not carry the same weight coming out of someone else's mouth. That is precisely why your voice matters. The narcissist was trying to parrot you by mocking your phrases, idioms, and colloquialisms, which is a silly attempt to copy you. Imitation may be the sincerest form of flattery, but some people botch the job and make a futile attempt at copying an original.

"It can be extremely tough emotionally to recover from any relationship, let alone one that was filled with mental abuse and confusion. Nothing was ever peaceful and steady; not when you stood up for yourself or tried to input boundaries. So, now you have taught yourself not to speak so much even when you need to. In that relationship you learned how to survive by not speaking your mind, by not having boundaries, by just doing what made the narcissist happy regardless of how it made you feel. – Jade Asikiwebe[46]

Now that you realize you are a voice in this world, nobody should silence you. It is a known fact that many operate out

46 Jade Asikiwe. *Overcoming Narcissistic Relationships as an Empath: Breaking the Karmic Cycles of Empaths and Narcissists.* Coppell, TX

of fear and love. What love will not motivate people to do, fear will. Furthermore, when you have been with someone who is not emotionally intelligent, lacks awareness or has an inability to regulate their emotions, get ready because you are going to live a life of stress which leads to illness and disease. Remember F.O.G. [Are you operating with them out of these three; Fear, Obligation, Guilt?] How?

The narcissist thinks they are right, and you are wrong. They are bothered by any hint of criticism or attempt to improve them because they know better than you. Because of this stance, your partner is angry, defensive, jealous, envious, persnickety, and triggered every time you speak. They are reactive and combative. They are dismissive of your feelings while demanding that you hear and adhere to theirs.

While this is happening before you, you get a clear and concise message that it is not safe for you to speak your truth. You cannot speak up for yourself because they will practice D.A.R.V.O. [deny, accuse, reverse-victim, offend] You then realize when you cannot speak your truth, you are dealing with a thief who has robbed you of opportunities to express yourself.

What do you do? You shut up so you can hear them, but they are not listening to you. You bite your tongue because they will play victim and you are wanting to come to a resolution, but they are seeking to manipulate and control. The reaction they give you will cause you to quiet down until you say nothing. It's damned if you do and damned if you don't. If you speak, you are a villain. If you do not speak, you are not communicating. If you take a break, you are lazy. If you get involved, you do too much. They keep you in the conundrum of emotional abandonment for your own truth. Your body is storing all that energy that you are not letting go of by speaking your truth.

Over time, your body swells. It is not the food and diet change, though that does have something to do with it. You are storing all the emotions from being silenced year after year after year. Speak your truth. But practice J.A.D.E. Do not try to Justify with a narcissist. Do not try to Argue with a narcissist. Do not Defend your position too strongly with a narcissist. Do not Explain too much to a narcissist.

It is written somewhere, 'know when to speak and when to be silent.' When you speak, people will listen. Even the narcissist listens. That is why they are triggered, angry, combative, and trying to silence you. They do not want to look within because that would mean they are wrong, and their fragile ego cannot handle any criticism of them for being wrong or needing to grow and mature. They tried to destroy you with smear campaigns, dog whistling, reverse smear campaigns, and lies by omission.

They heard you. They just feel they are right, and that means you should not be listened to. You can destroy them with facts, figures, and evidence to support your truth. You can destroy them with truth alone. As a matter of fact, you saved their reputation by not telling your side of the story. By not speaking your version of events, they were spared. If you told others what you had been through, it would make their hair stand up and goosebumps would cover them. If people understood narcissism, when they meet the narcissist and they see the tactic of them playing victim and coloring others badly, then they would know to let the narcissist talk and then find the person they are talking about and get their side of the story.

The narcissist does not want you to speak, because you will set the record straight and clear your name. When you do, you will invalidate them, expose them, and make them look bad. This is exactly what they want to avoid. They want to avoid the opposite of pride, which is shame.

It is time to reclaim your voice. A model experience for you is Maxine Waters, an American politician representing the state of California as the 43rd congressional district since 1991 and her questioning of Treasury Secretary Steven Mnuchin. She was speaking and asked the question, "Is there some reason why I did not get a response to the letter I sent on May 23?" (TS) Steven Mnuchin responded with, "Thank you," and other filibuster statements.

While Mr. Mnuchin was speaking, congressperson Maxine Waters responded to his response by saying, "Thank you very much. Reclaiming my time. Reclaiming my time. Reclaiming my time." No matter what he said, if it was not a straight answer to her question, she responded, "Reclaiming my time." "Reclaiming my time." The chairperson, Thomas Jeb Hensarling, spoke and said, "The time belongs to the gentlelady from California." Later Maxine Waters said, "Thank you for your compliments about how great I am, but

I don't want to waste my time on me."…"What he failed to tell you is when you're on my time, I can reclaim it." You must reclaim your time. You must reclaim your voice and the power of your words. Abracadabra – create as you speak. Think it, speak it, do it. I understand you may be used to letting others speak first.

You may be used to them overtalking you or even belittling your words you speak. But today, you are smarter than you were before. You realize that silence is just as loud as volume. Your insides are shouting for justice with a whisper that is very loud. You also know that actions speak louder than words. Speak up! And if they will not let you, find a way to get it out. Speak your truth. Reclaim your time.

Now is the time to heal that part of yourself that has been silenced. It is time to see the beauty and capabilities that you have. When you listen to someone you love and respect tell you for so long that you are not anything that you want or hope to be, you can sadly come to believe that it is true.

But the voice within is telling you, 'you are amazing. You are special. You are not wrong for having feelings of your own. You are not wrong for wanting to express that you feel some kind of way because the boundary that was set has been crossed. You are not crazy. You are conscious. You are cognizant.

You are aware and you have found your voice in the room.' Open that throat chakra and use your voice to speak affirmations over your life and put some feet on those affirmations with actions that reflect the same. That voice is telling you and guiding you to express yourself. That voice is your highest self saying, "I am tired of pretending to be all right with this toxic behavior.

I am miserable holding in my feelings so someone that I love can act like my feelings, words, thoughts, opinions, boundaries, and life does not matter to them." "I am tired of giving up the right for the wrong to cover the multitude of faults you have." "I am tired of letting you disrespect me with witty comments when you are the problem." And if they genuinely love you and respect you, there is no way in hell they can keep silencing you so they can feel okay. You have caught on to that trick and the magician has been discovered to be a con.

If you need help expressing yourself, take courage. We already know they are going to deflect, get angry, throw a temper tantrum, give you a narcissist rage, deny it, trigger you, react, lie, manipulate and gaslight you. Therefore, what is the worst that can happen that has not already happened? You can try journaling as a method to find your voice in the room. Journaling is very therapeutic.

When you write a journal, the journal allows you to express yourself with no judgement. You can write exactly how you feel at that moment and later go back and see how your feelings drive your actions. Never let the narcissist read your journal. This will only trigger them and cause them to try to counter and gaslight you for having thoughts and feelings of your own. The pages of the journal listen, hear you, remember you, respect you and are okay with you being your authentic self. Scribble, doodle, write one word or 5,000. But say what you have to say. Tell the truth, the whole truth, and nothing but the truth so help you.

Next, speak up for yourself. Speaking up for yourself means that you are deliberately choosing to say what you feel in the moment. And who gives a damn if they don't like you? Speak your opinion and speak out loud. It is so much better to be hated for who you are than loved for who you're not.

The narcissist is skilled at deflecting, reversing the blame and using their victim consciousness to cleverly confuse you. They may answer your question with a question to keep you off balance. Elizabeth Perry, ACC offers a few helpful tips for someone needing to speak up for themselves.

◊ Understand that saying no can be a good thing
◊ Emulate words with your body's posture
◊ Stay true to your words
◊ Practice when you can
◊ Consider how you could be giving too much
◊ Know when to leave the relationship!
◊ Take your time with your response(s)
◊ Remind yourself that you deserve respect[47]

Speaking up for yourself and others is when you communicate publicly, assertively, and honestly for rights and needs. Though the narcissist is committed to misunderstanding you and keeping confusion and chaos going, you will need to

---

47   Elizabeth Perry, ACC. *One Life Skill Everybody needs: Learn how to stand up for yourself.* April 5, 2022. https://www.betterup.com/blog/how-to-stand-up-for-yourself

speak truth and power. At its heart, speaking up for yourself and others is really a conversation regarding boundaries. The narcissist has probably conditioned you to second-guess everything and not speak up because you downplay an issue as not a big deal. When you feel that you need to speak up, you instinctively feel that a boundary or value that you hold has been violated in some way. However, the desire to reinforce the boundary comes into conflict with another value: the desire to be accepted.[48]

You are trying to be heard and establish boundaries. They are using the Miranda rights move on you. The conflict you probably feel is cognitive dissonance. You feel you should say something but you also feel like it will fall on deaf ears. You establish boundaries and they disregard them. You set rules and order. They usurp the authority.

A part of you is saying, 'What is the point in speaking up if they are going to just do the same things anyway?' The point is, you are a voice in this world, damnit! You just happen to be in a toxic relationship with a narcissist who cannot handle the truth that they are the cause of their own misery. They cannot handle being wrong. And if truth be told, they are not right all the time or most of it either.

I personally do not think you were stupid for loving the narcissist. I think you were brave. In spite of all the warning signs, red flags, and unconventional behavior, you loved hard.

---

48 Allaya Cooks-Campbell. *Speaking up for yourself is important – 11 Steps to get it right. May 20, 2021.* https://www.betterup.com/blog/speaking-up-for-yourself

Though you gave love to the wrong person, you gave until you had nothing left. You were selfless. And that does not make you weak. It makes you brave. You loved a broken person who pretended to be something and someone they were not. And the best thing to come out of that was you learned to love yourself. You learned to study yourself and feel your feelings. You also learned to not take the disrespect. Congratulations.

If you have to sacrifice your voice "to keep the peace" it's no longer peaceful. You're internalizing the chaos instead.

~Zara Bas

CHAPTER 23

10 PHRASES THAT CAN DISARM THE NARCISSIST

Narcissists have a way of making other people feel guilty and using fear and intimidation to control people. However, you should think about what the narcissist is trying to use to get out of you. Here is Fear, Obligation and Guilt. (F.O.G.) in action. You may be thinking, 'am I going to get in trouble for standing up for myself?' No matter what, you must call it out in a non-confrontational way. This disarms them. The fear and intimidating behavior may not always be physical. Sometimes it's psychological.

The F.O.G. are used to create threats of abandonment, rejection, infidelity, and withholding love and affection from the narcissist. The obligation may come at the cost of them creating bonding obligations whereby they make the unsuspecting victim feel indebted to them because of something they have done. Debt makes a slave of the borrower.

That is an adage as old as time. The guilt kicks in and the victim feels an obligation to fulfill their demands, both small and large, and disregard their own needs and desires because they owe them. Nevertheless, you can call it out by saying, "I heard what you said, but maybe you didn't mean it that way. What did you mean?"

If you find yourself in an argument or confrontation with a narcissist, Alana Carvalho LMHC suggests some phrases that can help you disarm them. She also explains how each of these phrases can help you diffuse the situation and disengage from it.[49]

"That doesn't work for me."

It is important to speak up for yourself and let them know if you are not OK with what they have decided.

"I can understand how you feel, but I feel differently."

You do not need to try to prove who is right or wrong. You can feel and see a situation differently and that is fine. Trying to prove your point will give them more ammunition to use against you.

"I don't see myself that way."

Often, narcissists will try to make themselves feel better by making you feel negatively about yourself.[4] It is important that you stay strong in what you believe is true.

---

49   Sandra Holbrook. Stand Up for Yourself: 10 Phrases to disarm a Narcissist. https://www.verywellmind.com/10-phrases-to-disarm-a-narcissist

"I remember it differently."

This is especially important when a narcissist is telling you that you might be imagining something or that it never happened. Let them know that you remember what really happened so they cannot manipulate events. Do not let them make you doubt yourself.

"I will only have a conversation with you about this if you're willing to listen and try to understand my perspective."

Setting boundaries for the conversation upfront can help ensure that the conversation is more respectful. Otherwise, you do not have to discuss that particular subject with them.

"I'm not going to explain why this is important to me, but it is."

Sometimes, we need to put a boundary in place with a narcissist, but we have to be mindful that when we explain why, it gives them an opportunity to manipulate or gaslight us. In such situations, you can uphold what is important to you without giving big explanations.

"I'm not willing to talk about that."

If a narcissist brings up a subject that they know you don't want to talk about, it's important to <u>assert</u> that you're not willing to engage with them. You do not have to justify your reasons for not wanting to discuss it.

"If you continue to speak to me like that, I will walk away."

If the conversation is becoming <u>toxic</u>, you need to make it clear that you will not tolerate their disrespect. State your boundaries clearly and firmly.

"I'm going to step away from this conversation."

It is important to stick to your boundaries. Realize when you need to disengage and step away to get clarity.

"Thank you for inviting me, but I'm not available."

If you want to sever contact with the narcissist, politely but firmly let them know that you are not available or interested.[50]

---

50   Sanjana Gupta. Reviewed by Sabrina Romanoff, PsyD. Use These 10 Phrases to Disarm a Narcissist. https://www.verywellmind.com/10-phrases-to-disarm-a-narcissis

Bonus phrase

"I see right through you"

When you tell a narcissist "I see right through you," you're essentially piercing through their carefully constructed façade. This statement can trigger a range of reactions, all driven by their need to maintain their self-image. Telling a narcissist "I see right through you" can have a profound impact on both parties involved. While it can trigger defensive and aggressive reactions from the narcissist, it can also empower the confronter. It's a declaration of awareness; a testament to the clarity and discernment of the speaker.

To confront a narcissist with such a potent statement, it is crucial to be prepared for the potential fallout. Narcissists thrive on control and admiration, and exposing their vulnerabilities can lead to unpredictable reactions.

The magic of words is they have power to do more than convey meaning; not only do they have the power to make things clear, but they also make things happen.
~Frederick Buechner

CHAPTER 24

THE POSTLOGUE

ONE LAST THING YOU SHOULD KNOW.

The narcissist may not hate you. However, what they may hate is that you no longer buy into the fantasy world they attempted to create. What they hate is that you are no longer under their spell and cannot be controlled and manipulated so easily. They hate that you saw through them and their façade and actually loved them for the person they showed you they were. What they hate is that when they look at you, they are reminded of how super selfish they are.

They hate that you learned to love yourself, something they cannot seem to do for themselves. When they look at you, they are reminded of the uncalled-for lies they told. They are reminded of their gaslighting. They are reminded of the façade they have tried tirelessly to keep up. They are reminded of the karma they are going to get for doing you wrong when your intentions were pure but theirs were selfish. When they see you, they remember their triangulation, unfaithfulness, and moments when they were unfaithful for no other reason than they are selfish as a human being.

When they see you, they are reminded of how they self-sabotage themselves and how you find ways to bounce back, thus exposing their immaturity and lack of ability to achieve. When they look at you, they are reminded of just how much they needed you to function. That is frustrating to that egomaniacal maniac.

When they see you, they realize you discovered their biggest weakness; the fact that they are never happy with the person they were with every day, themselves. They know that you know they are never satisfied and never happy. They do not appreciate what they have.

They are always searching for something even when they have something good. Their grass is green, but they thought someone else's grass was greener. They never feel complete and are always trying to escape the feelings of that emptiness. They will always find something wrong with you. They may even devote themselves to letting you know something wrong about you daily in order to avoid their own inadequacy.

This is why they are impossible to live with or be with. They are not satisfied with what they have and try to find greener pastures with each new partner. When they see you, they see how grotesquely evil their heart is, and they do not like looking within because it causes them pain. Looking at you supremely disrupts the fantasy world they live in. Staying with you after disrespecting you disrupts the fantasy narrative; they are trying to convince you and everyone else that they are the good thing.

When they look at you after sticking around so long, they are reminded of how even after they tried to clone you, rob you and parasite off you, they still did not get it right. You are the real McCoy, and they are a phony cheap copy. When you hold them accountable for their behavior, it triggers their shame [which is exactly what they are trying to avoid] and the feelings of guilt they do not want to see.

They were arrogant and prideful when doing the things they did, but because they have been exposed they feel the shame of the effects of the consequences of their actions. They cannot take the onslaught of shame. That is why they pushed you away. That is why they reverse discarded you. By treating you badly, it allows them to practice the reverse discard by letting you be the one to end it and then they can play the victim again in the story they are rehearsing for future supply.

They cannot deal with you as a healed, aware empath because they cannot deal with themselves. Remember, this is not about you. Neither is it personal towards you. They are still trying to argue with you because winning against you at all costs gives them a reward, but you are no longer arguing with them. You are passive and they do not know how to handle the art of war that your silence brings to them. Them cheating on you had everything to do with the emptiness they feel from the insatiable appetite for attention that cannot be filled. Them stealing your identity and doing white-collar crimes is just another way of them getting supply. Them having a private life you know little to nothing about is just them being a fake, fraud, and relationship chameleon. The narcissist will continue down their dark corridors of life never feeling whole, complete, or satisfied with anything or anyone. They are stuck being a child trapped in an aging adult body and angst is coming and has already come.

If they were to ever change sincerely, which they probably will not, they would have to be honest. They would have to be introspective, be contrite, repent and say, "I did wrong." "I'm not right." "I did them wrong." Their ego will likely not let them do that, since they think they are always right and know better than you.

This kind of thinking equals no growth. No change. It causes them to stay stuck in the same egocentric, self-destructive behavior for life because it lacks accountability. Simply put, they will reap what they sow. The seed is corruption and the fruit is the destruction of everything they put their hands on.

The question is, is the narcissist willing to put in the work of self-reflection and humility and admitting that they do not know everything? Next, are they willing to accept that learning from mistakes is how to repair conflict and heal the damage that they have caused from invalidation or gaslighting or lying or selfishness? One of the most destructive traits of a narcissist is the inability to take any accountability. Acknowledging wrongs is only the admission of the act [not guilt for the narcissist], but fixing what was broken and messed up is true accountability. The narcissists are always the victims and are stuck in victim consciousness, which causes their ego to not handle the shame of admitting that they are capable of making a mistake or doing something wrong. A major reason narcissistic relationships are so toxic and damaging is because of their self-centeredness.

Next, their pride and egos are incompatible with closeness and connection. It is not easy to have intimacy or mutual respect or emotional safety with someone who thinks that they are superior to you, more special, or entitled to what they will not give to you, and who tries to dominate, manipulate, or control you.

Beloved, you will never feel safe with someone who purposely violates your boundaries, lies habitually, or invalidates and dismisses your feelings. Furthermore, you will never feel connected to someone who refuses to accept constructive feedback without punishing you for offering it.

People that love each other every day require so much more than love by itself. Real love requires being inconvenienced sometimes, not all the time. Relationships require mutual respect and consideration and affection and gentleness and the ability to empathize. Which the narcissist cannot give or be. So, can a narcissist change? Absolutely! Anyone can change. The question is, are they willing to put in the work?

Please understand, there is nothing you could have done more or less of to save the relationship with the narcissist. That narcissist was at war inwardly. They hate themselves to the core and cannot accept real love no matter how much you try to give it to them. As it is written earlier, they are like children stuck in adult bodies. They want to grow up so badly but because they cannot self-reflect on how they are the problem, they never grow up. They do not know how to validate themselves and are stuck constantly seeking attention and affection. The need is insatiable and unsatisfiable.

The need encompasses their whole life. They are always chasing supply in the form of attention, reaction, and control through the use of manipulation. No matter how much you give and give, the void inside them cannot be filled. Nothing you do is ever going to be enough. What they truly seek is inward and not external. But no partner, person, parent, friend, colleague, associate or even a god can give that to them.

They have to look within and they do not want to look within because they will feel the shame. They do not want to take ownership that they are not all they think they are. The problem is, they do not see that they leave a lot to be desired. Then they blame others, deny the wounds, and keep repeating the same damaging cycle; Love bomb, hook, devalue, discard, hoover and repeat with you and the new or an old supply.

Armed with this information, no, you could not have saved the relationship. You were never the problem. You simply loved someone who could not be reached. Once they found your replacement, everything you do starts to annoy them even the simple things they used to claim to love. That's how you know it is already over. Let it be over.

Remember this - you must be something special for them to try to be you in another body. You must be something special for them to not like their original self and have to tear you down. You are a badass in a human body. They know this. Now you do too. Begin your healing journey and become the best version of you.

TERMS AND DEFINITIONS

Below are terms and definitions associated with narcissistic behavior.

Arrested development – When trauma impairs your ability to develop full emotional maturity, this is known as arrested psychological development. Trauma can "freeze" your emotional response at the age you experienced it.

Baiting - In the psychological sense, baiting occurs when someone intentionally acts in a way to elicit, trigger, or provoke an emotional response from whoever they are interacting with. In this case, the narcissistic parent attempts to "bait" their child. Baiting is often used when one person wants to start an argument or some kind of conflict with another person.[51]

Betrayal – This is the act or fact of violating someone's trust or confidence, of breaking a moral standard, or of revealing something hidden or secret.

Blind Support – We see behaviors of the narcissist that do not match our expectations, and we still support them knowing they do not have our best interests at heart. The empath is honest, loyal, and devoted, and the narcissist knows this - thus they take advantage of the empath's kindness as a weakness. Often the victim is a perfectionist. A previous relationship with a narcissist had a lot of goalpost moving and to get it right means so much. So, blindly you support,

---

51   Author unknown: *7 Types of Narcissistic Baiting and How to Deal with it.* Https://hopefulpanda.com/narcissistic-baiting/ Taken 12/22/23.

because no second-guessing comes from this behavior except second-guessing your actions and motives.

Boundaries – These are a code of conduct or an unwritten set of rules which we consider to be reasonable behavior from those around us, and we will have our own response when someone steps over the line.

Breadcrumbing – Breadcrumbing means someone leads another person on by dropping small tidbits of interest—such as social media interactions, occasional messages, or brief phone calls. These interactions are intended to suggest the person is still interested, but they occur sporadically, and there is generally no intention of following through.[52] This involves a small-but-inconsistent supply of interest that keeps someone feeling as though there is the potential for more. Narcissists may breadcrumb you with occasional and inconsistent sex, cooking, money, resources, love, affection, assistance, support for your dreams, and moral decency. By the time you get what you want, you are so happy to get it that you fail to realize the breadcrumbs are tools for manipulation.

Brain Fog – Brain fog is not a medical condition. However, the term is used to describe the feeling of being mentally sluggish and fuzzy. Brain fog feels like a lack of mental clarity; it can affect your ability to focus and make it difficult for you to recall things. Narcissists often use word

---

52 Macmillan Dictionary. Definition of breadcrumbing, buzzword from Macmillan dictionary.

salad, lies, denial, future faking, and deflection to cause a victim to develop brain fog.

Bullying – When done by a narcissist, this is a distinctive pattern of repeatedly and deliberately harming and humiliating others - specifically those who are smaller, weaker, younger or in any way more vulnerable than the bully. The grandiose narcissist is associated with bullying which typically falls into six categories, some of which are more obvious than others. These categories include physical bullying, verbal bullying, relational bullying, cyberbullying, sexual bullying, and prejudicial bullying.

Codependent Relationship - This is a dysfunctional relationship dynamic where one person assumes the role of "the giver," sacrificing their own needs and well-being for the sake of the other, "the taker." The bond in question does not have to be romantic; it can occur just as easily between parent and child, friends, and family members.[53] The givers are often more self-critical and often perfectionistic; fixing things or helping and rescuing others makes them feel needed. Nobody needs help more than a narcissist that cannot get their act together.

Complex Post Traumatic Stress Disorder C-PTSD – This is an anxiety condition that involves many of the same symptoms of PTSD, along with other symptoms. It can be caused by long-term repeated trauma. Symptoms include, but are not limited to: (1) Difficulty controlling emotions.

---

53 https://www.psychologytoday.com/us/basics/codependency   taken 12/11/2023.

(2) Negative self-view. (3) Difficulty with relationships. (4) Detachment from the trauma. (5) Loss of a system of meanings. [losing hope, faith, and values].

Cognitive dissonance – This occurs when one holds two or more contradictory beliefs or values at the same time. Sometimes people hold extraordinarily strong beliefs and, when they are presented with evidence which opposes those beliefs, they find it impossible to accept evidence to the contrary. You probably cannot believe that they would betray, cheat, lie, manipulate, and do the things they do to you to hurt and abuse you since you think they love you.

Compassion Fatigue – This is also known as secondary or vicarious trauma, and it's prolonged exposure to other people's trauma, abuse, or misuse of your time trust and energy. This form of fatigue can cause a loss of empathetic feeling, and your own feelings of being trapped and helplessness with a sense of burnout. It is also a form of traumatic stress resulting from repeated exposure to traumatized individuals, or aversive details of traumatic events while working in a helping or protecting profession. This indirect form of trauma exposure differs from experiencing trauma oneself. Symptoms of compassion fatigue can include, but are not limited to, exhaustion, insomnia, sleep deprivation anxiety, headaches, upset stomach, long-term irritability, numbness, a decline in one's sense of purpose, emotional detachments, self-contempt, and self-gaslighting. When dealing with narcissists, you are likely to develop compassion fatigue.

Dark Empath – often described as the worse nightmare of a narcissist, is an individual that can understand and recognize the emotions of others but uses this ability to manipulate and exploit them rather than help. In contrast to typical empaths, the dark empath uses charm and charisma as a tool to leverage their understanding of emotions to gain control, exploit vulnerabilities, develop emotional bonds that they can use or as an advantage of the situation for their perceived benefit.

D.A.R.V.O. – an acronym that stands for Deny, Attack, Reverse-Victim, Offend. The narcissist will deny any wrongdoing. Then they will attack you. When you defend yourself, they will reverse it and play victim and speak and offend. Clever tactic, but only when you are not aware of the games.

Dry begging –This is indirectly asking for something or subtly implying it. Dropping vague hints which are not clear or straightforward when making a request. It is making a suggestion that usually appeals to the victim's emotions. Dry begging is known as a manipulative tactic used by covert narcissists. It elicits attention, provokes sympathy, and acquires resources while maintaining a façade of humility and need. i.e., "Some shrimp would be nice right now." "I wish I could get a bouquet of flowers from somewhere. I never get flowers." "I am short on my rent, and I do not know what I am going to do." After they do this and you give it to them, they will likely say, "I never asked you to do this!"

Devaluing – The devaluation phase is the second stage of the narcissist's abuse cycle. The narcissist will begin using passive-aggression as indirect aggression. They may start with snarky remarks about your weight, put-downs on your intelligence when you make simple mistakes, twisting your words/taking things out of context on purpose, hinting at insults or negativity, gaslighting, sarcasm, false or backhanded compliments, playing mind games, and making excuses for all their failures and shortcomings. In short, they are attempting to lessen your value in your own mind's eye.

Discard (Narcissistic) – This is the phase in which the narcissist distances themselves from or ends a relationship with their supply once they no longer perceive the other person as useful or capable of fulfilling their needs. They may become distant, cold, or unresponsive to your needs. They may demean, belittle, or criticize you. They may ignore or refuse to engage with you and even ignore all other attempts to communicate. The discard may happen suddenly without warning or explanation.

Delusions of grandeur – These happen when one has a false belief about one's own greatness or skills. Narcissists may express this by giving an overinflated sense of their self or self-worth. They may claim to be close to celebrities, public officials, and people of importance. They will sell the idea that they are important to a community.

Dog Whistling – In the context of abusive relationships, dog whistling can be used to target and terrorize the victim. Narcissistic and psychopathic individuals can use insidious and diverse forms of dog whistling to covertly manipulate and belittle their victims while escaping consequences, accountability, and judgment from others. Narcissists and psychopaths can use abusive "dog whistles" in public to subtly degrade and threaten you in front of others, to compare you to others, or even use them in one-on-one conversations with you where the intention is to gaslight, taunt, mock and slander you, should you try to call them out for their behavior. Here are some common ways they may use "dog whistling" to covertly abuse you: **1)** Degrading you in front of others to underhandedly humiliate you. 2) Dishing out covert threats. **3)** Covertly abusing, retraumatizing and gaslighting you one-on-one by making references to your past traumas, wounds, and triggers. **4)** Making subtle, degrading comparisons and inducing jealousy and 5) Provoking you through social media.

Empath – Someone who is sensitive to the emotions and feelings of others.[54]

Empathy – The ability to understand the experiences and feelings of others outside of your own perspective.

Enabler – This is someone who, by their action or inaction, encourages or enables a pattern of behavior to continue or remove consequences of unruly behavior. If you are reading this, you probably were the enabler in the relationship with the narcissist.

---

54 Murphy, Victor. *Highly Sensitive Empaths and Narcissists: The Empath's survival guide to healing from Toxic Relationship. Discover your skills, understanding your gift, and stop being a victim of Narcissistic Abuse.* USA. 2019.

Flying Monkeys – Flying monkeys are people who have been convinced by the narcissist that he or she is the real victim. They inflict further harm on the real victim by submitting to the narcissist's wishes and demands. They may threaten, torment, discredit or add fuel to a smear campaign by spreading lies and gossip.

Freudian Slip – This is an unintentional error in speech regarded as revealing subconscious feelings. Aka: a slip of the tongue.

Faux Apology – This is a statement in the form of an apology that does not express remorse for what was done or said, or which assigns fault to those ostensibly receiving the apology. i.e., I am sorry if you feel…I am sorry that you…. I know that I …. I will apologize if you never bring it up….x told me to apologize…. sorry, not sorry…. I regret…. I was just….

F.O.G. – Acronym for Fear, Obligation and Guilt. The narcissist will try to use fear to intimidate you, bully you or make you afraid of what may happen. Next they trap you in a no-win situation with obligations. They know you are a person of integrity and will do what is right so they close out the games with guilt.

Future faking – This happens when the narcissist makes promises of change or creating a bright future, only to remain the same and never amount to anything. They will sell you a dream of waking up in the clouds and yet days, weeks, months, years, and decades later, you will end up in the dirt. This method is used to draw you in and keep you engrossed in the relationship. They discuss future plans with you like a wedding, having children, vacations, opening a business, spending your golden years together. With this style of conversation, they fool you into believing they will be with you for the long haul.

Gaslighting – This is the practice of psychologically manipulating someone into questioning their own sanity, memory, or powers of reasoning. Examples include trivializing what matters to you, playing the devil's advocate, stonewalling to end a conversation, accusing you of being overly sensitive, shifting the blame to avoid accountability, projecting their faults onto you, pretending to have allies, comparing you to others, and using indignant outrage.

Goalpost moving – This is a metaphor derived from goal-based sports, which means to change the rule or criterion (goal) of a process or competition while it is still in progress, in such a way that the new goal offers one side an advantage or disadvantage.[55] Narcissists often do this to keep you second-guessing. You may feel that nothing is ever good enough when this is being done to you.

Goldbricking – This is the practice of doing less work than one is able to, while maintaining the appearance of working. A goldbricker is an individual who seeks to get paid a wage or salary for work that is not done, despite the appearance of being industrious.

---

55 https://en.wikipedia.org/wiki/Moving_the_goalposts

Golden Child – A narcissistic parent's favorite child. This child is idealized as perfect and special. The parent projects all the positive qualities of this golden child and brags about his or her wonderful accomplishments to anyone who will listen.[56]

Grey Rock – This is a tactic some people use when dealing with abusive or manipulative behavior. It involves becoming as uninteresting and unengaged as possible so that the other person loses interest.

Hoovering – The term hoovering is used in relationships to represent the vacuuming up of happiness, positivity, and optimism that the other partner may be experiencing. It also refers intentional behavior made by the narcissist to bring their victim back into their life.

Idealization – This stage is also known as the appreciation stage, and it is typically characterized by love bombing. This is where the narcissist showers the person with attention and affection. The narcissist creates a sense of instant connection with you. They make you feel unique and wonderful, and put you up on a pedestal. Regardless of the type of relationship they participate in - romantic, parent, child, friendly, professional, or otherwise — it moves fast and has a fervent quality to it.

Isolation – Narcissists isolate their partners by monopolizing their time, undermining other relationships,

---

56   https://www.psychologytoday.com/ca/blog/understanding-narcissism/201909/understanding-the-terms-narcissism

and controlling communication and finances to create dependency and cut off support networks.[57]

Invalidation – Invalidation is a manipulative tactic used to get a target to believe that their thoughts, opinions, and beliefs are wrong, unimportant, or do not matter. Narcissists are good at using this tactic. They may do this by finding out all you want, not giving it to you, then giving it to someone else and making sure you find out about it. They may even give you everything, then withdraw it and deem you unworthy of receiving it from them, then give those very things to someone else right in front of your eyes.

J.A.D.E. –Justify Argue Defend Explain. Do not do these things with a narcissist if you can avoid it. Arguing with a narcissist only leads to them avoiding all accountability and responsibility and justifying themselves.

Love bombing – a term used to describe the typical initial stages of a relationship with a narcissistic personality where the narcissist goes all out to impress their target with flattery, holidays, and promises of a future together, having the target believe that they have met their perfect partner; their soulmate.[58]

Mental midget – Because narcissists often have arrested development, many of them are mental midgets. They are people with fragile mindsets and lack the ability to deal with

---

57   https://thenarcissisticlife.com/how-do-narcissists-isolate-their-partners-from-family-and-friends/ taken 1/22/2024.
58   https://themindsjournal.com/twenty-common-terms-in-the-world-of-narcissism/ taken 12/10/2023.

tough situations. They may ask for your advice and then turn down your advice. Yet, someone else will give the exact same advice and they will listen and implement the advice from someone else.

Mirroring – A narcissist will mirror what they see in you - from your mannerisms to your dress sense, your behavior and your likes and dislikes. They basically become just like you.

Monkey Branching – Monkey branching is when someone in a committed monogamous relationship begins dating other people while still in their current relationship.[59] Someone who's monkey branching will be texting, calling, flirting, and even going on dates with people who are not their partner.

Narcissistic Collapse – This is defined as a massive mental breakdown that occurs when and if the narcissist loses the primary source of supply. The death of the spouse, child, or whoever, or whatever the supply is for them. The collapse of the false self is inevitable because the major supply is no longer available to help hide the façade and buffer as the camouflage suit.

Narcissistic Injury – Narcissistic injury, also called narcissistic wound or wounded ego, is known as the defensive mechanisms in the form of reaction to the emotional trauma that the narcissist feels or perceives when they are overwhelmed because they feel their pride and self-worth

---

59   Bijan Kholghi. What is Monkey Branching? 20 Clear signs and what to do (2025). http://www.coaching-online.cor/monkey-branching/

have been devastated. It also refers to any perceived threat to a narcissist's self-esteem or self-worth, though none are apparent. The injury can occur when the narcissist feels judged, criticized, ignored, humiliated, exposed, or not given the attention they believe they deserve. Narcissistic injury can lead to feelings of emptiness, insecurity, inferiority, and unlovability that can have long-term consequences for the individual if not addressed.

Narcissistic Leveling – Leveling refers to the disturbed narcissist's attempt to put themselves on equal standing with others of different character. It generally takes two forms: setting oneself up as a person of equal stature to a person in authority; and trying to equate one's own character, personal value, integrity, etc. with someone else's, especially someone of more mature or superior character. It is a slick way to try and 'level the playing field' or field of interpersonal contest.[60] Examples include phrases like, "You're not perfect" "Are you saying you're better than me?" "Are you saying that I don't do my part." "I embarrassed you?! What about the time you did this and such?"

Narcissistic Mask – Narcissists have several versions of themselves who they show at different times depending on who they are with. This is why their friends see one version of them, but you see a totally different version of them behind

---

60 Victoria. Unmasking the Narc. https://unmaskingthenarc.com/narcissist-gaslighting-phrases/

closed doors. Narcissists know exactly which 'mask' to wear based on who they are with and what they are wanting.[61]

Narcissistic Personality Disorder – This is a mental health condition characterized by an unrealistic sense of self-importance, an excessive need for praise, and other traits that negatively impact one's relationships, self-image, and daily life. It can also be defined by a sense of grandiosity, a continuous desire for admiration, arrogance, and fantasies of unlimited power and success— this is the most classic type. Other types of narcissism have been described, including covert, antagonistic, communal, malignant, maladaptive, and adaptive.[62] This personality disorder is associated with the following characteristics: (a) a long-standing pattern of grandiose self-importance and an exaggerated sense of talent and achievements; (b) fantasies of unlimited sex, power, brilliance, or beauty; (c) an exhibitionistic need for attention and admiration; (d) either cool indifference or feelings of rage, humiliation, or emptiness as a response to criticism, indifference, or defeat; and (e) various interpersonal disturbances, such as feeling entitled to special favors, taking advantage of others, and inability to empathize with the feelings of others.[63]

---

61   Erica Randle. Narcissism Terminology| You're A-Z Guide https://shecounselling.com.au/narcissism-terminology-your-a-z-guide/ taken 1/23/24.

62   https://www.verywellhealth.com/narcissistic-personality-disorder-types-5213256 taken 12/11/2023.

63   https://dictionary.apa.org/narcissistic-personality-disorder Taken 12/11/2023.

Narcissistic Supply – Narcissists are bottomless pits for having their needs met. If you get in a relationship with a narcissist, they expect you to supply them on some, if not all, levels. The supply they desire is insatiable. One person cannot fill all the needs, therefore they have a host or team of external validation parties to give supply. Narcissistic supply consists of attention, admiration, respect, adulation and even fear. Supply for the narcissist may be pathological or excessive. They often get this supply from codependents and the new victims. They are almost always in search of supply. Without these vital nutrients of life, the narcissist will become more dysfunctional. A narcissist is lost without narcissistic supply. They need supply like a plant needs water.

Narcissistic Rage – NPD people may react with narcissistic rage when they are not given the attention that they feel they deserve. This rage may take the form of screaming and yelling. Selective silence and passive-aggressive avoidance can also happen with narcissistic rage.

No Contact – No contact is a self-imposed set of rules whereby there will be absolutely no contact with the narcissistic or toxic person, (No texts, no emails, no phone calls, no snooping on social media). It has been likened to building a wall between you and a toxic individual. You will not care or even be aware of what happens on the other side of this wall. (Minimal contact is advised in circumstances where one has to co-parent with a narcissist).

Overtalking – a narcissist will often cause people to feel muted because the narcissist overtalks you and makes you second-guess yourself, thus causing you to not feel heard or validated. You may often find, if you are aware, that you talk a lot - especially to someone who will listen - because the narcissist silenced you on so many other occasions.

Passive-aggressive behaviors – Narcissistic passive-aggressive behavior is a way of expressing pent-up hostility and their sense of superiority covertly. A passive-aggressive narcissist may gaslight, manipulate, distort, make jokes, shift blame, and even belittle others, all in an attempt to punish them, control them, or seek revenge. They may utilize narcissistic rage or contemptable actions when they feel slighted, are told "no", or do not receive preferential treatment.

P.H.I.L. – **This is** an acronym that stands for Protector/ Provider. Helper/Hero. Integrity. Love/Loyalty.

Pyrrhic Victory – relating to a victory that is not worth winning because the winner has lost so much in winning it. More simply, winning costs so much that you lose the respect of the ones you defeat. Narcissists must win at all costs. During the devaluing stages they do not care that their tactics will cost them it is about winning for them. Even if they are wrong and it costs them everything to win, they must win.

Reactive abuse – when being abused by the narcissist, the one being abused might eventually reach the breaking point and lash out at their abuser in return. This usually is when the victim defends themselves by responding to the abuse with physical and verbal action or aggression to stop the abuse. The action may include, yelling, screaming, insulting, or even assaulting the narcissistic abuser.

Red Flags – Red flags are warning signs that something is not right, and often even if they are seen early in the relationship, people downplay them because they believe they are in love. Often they are only seen in retrospect - once the abuse has already commenced, seeing the red flags is often the saddest moment of awakening for a victim. Classic narcissistic red flags are an overinflated sense of self, lying, saying 'I love you' way too soon, their crisis becomes your emergency, triangulation with people they will not let go of, goldbricking, love bombing, arrogance, lack of respect for your boundaries etc.

Red herring – This is something that misleads or distracts from a relevant or important question. It may be either a logical fallacy or a literary device that leads readers or audiences toward a false conclusion. A red herring may be used intentionally, as in mystery fiction, or as part of rhetorical strategies (e.g., in politics), or may be used in argumentation inadvertently.[64]

Reverse Discard – This is a calculated move by the narcissist to retain control over their victim. Rather than severing ties completely, the narcissist engages in a cycle of intermittent reinforcement, oscillating between moments of closeness and withdrawal. This creates a psychological dependency within the victim, making it incredibly challenging to break free from the toxic relationship.[65] The

---

64   Oxford English Dictionary. OED Third Edition, September 2009. Taken 2/11/2024.

65   https://www.stopavoidingyourself.com/post/the-narcissist-s-reverse-

objective is to treat you so badly that you want out, thus they can play the victim and label you the bad guy since you left/ broke up with them.

Reverse Smear Campaign – The deliberate and calculated effort by the narcissist to use their harsh words and passive aggressive attitude to privately tarnish your reputation, credibility, or character. This is not constructive criticism, which is there to improve/grow you. This is when the narcissist tries to benefit from being associated with your greatness publicly, but cannot stand you privately. It is probably in the best interests of the narcissist not to not try to publicly smear your name if your character and reputation are solid, as they would face an immediate backlash by the people who know your reputation to be solid. The narcissist knows you are respected by your family and community; therefore, they will try to privately destroy you while giving the appearance of being a loving and devoted person to you. Also see dog whistling.

Pathological Envy – [also known as green envy] is known as a deeply rooted destructive form of envy. This type of envy is associated with NPD and is seen where individuals experience intense and often unwarranted feelings of resentment towards others particularly their perceived success or acquisition of possessions. The person with this envy feels envy because the person they envy "has something that they seem to lack," and that they are somehow entitled to whatever they envies, even if they have not earned it or labored for it

discard-revealing-their-manipulative-tactics

in any way. The envy is fueled by a perceived need to control because they feel they must diminish, negate or outshine the achievements of others to make themselves feel better.

Parroting – This happens when the narcissist finds a new person and they begin to repeat and imitate exactly what they say or do, without understanding it or thinking about what it means. Their paramour or person they are attempting to clone has an attractiveness about them they want, so they imitate them in every way imaginable.

Projection – this is a defense mechanism used by narcissists to cope with their own feelings of inadequacy or insecurity by attributing these negative traits to others. They often accuse you of the things that they are feeling, experiencing, or doing. They often shift responsibility or shame for something they have done or are not able to do onto someone else. One of the biggest is to accuse you of only thinking about yourself, which is exactly what they are doing.

Provocative Victim – A person that provokes behavior in another person then twists the narrative when they are being held accountable for the role they played in the situation. They often act or behave in ways that arouse negative responses from others close to them. These responses include anger, irritation, and exasperation. Often, they are trying to maintain what is in fact a rather exaggerated sense of self-importance and entitlement for their peers.[66]

---

66 Baumeister, R. F., Bushman, B. J., & Campbell, W. K. (2000). Self-esteem, narcissism, and aggression: Does violence result from low self-esteem or from threatened egotism? *Current Directions in Psychological*

Scapegoat – as it relates to narcissists, the scapegoat is blamed for just about everything that goes wrong. All sins, mistakes and ill are put upon them as others shift the blame. The scapegoat is usually the one who can see through the façade and calls the narcissist out on the games being played.

Scapegoat Child – A child in a family may be singled out and subjected to unwarranted negative treatment. This child is the object of all the narcissistic parent's negative projections. He or she is devalued and treated as an insignificant loser who is blamed for everything that goes wrong, including things that are clearly other people's fault.[67]

Selective amnesia memory – Telling you something then denying ever saying it. Perhaps the narcissist will seem to just not remember certain events, and this will trigger you and cause you to get angry. Understand that this is a form of gaslighting you to provoke a response.

Self-Aware Narcissist - Self-awareness is a complex and multifaceted concept, involving an individual's ability to reflect on and understand their own thoughts, feelings, and behaviors. In the case of NPD, self-awareness may involve an individual recognizing that their thoughts, feelings, and behaviors are consistent with the symptoms of NPD. It is important to note that self-awareness does not necessarily lead to behavior change or treatment-seeking. However, self-

---

Science, 9(1), 26–29.

67 https://www.psychologytoday.com/ca/blog/understanding-narcissism/201909/understanding-the-terms-narcissism

awareness is often a necessary first step in recognizing the need for treatment and making positive changes in one's life.

Self-Gaslight – when you have been with a narcissist, often you self-gaslight. You hear a voice within that says, "Maybe this is my fault; maybe I could have done more." But snap out of that. Remember you gave your all and they still did what they did. You were self-sacrificing, loving, giving, and willing to help, but they were using you, they were goldbricking you, they were playing the victim. You did your best. You gave your all. You gave more than they reciprocated. While you were giving and doing, remember they were cheating, lying, stealing, misappropriating money, guilt-tripping and blame-shifting to make you feel bad about their dysfunction.

Smear Campaign – Narcissists attempts at tarnishing their victim's image and reputation and destroying their self-esteem and sense of reality. The smear campaign is born out of a combination of factors, including the need to be right and have his or her "truth" become the prevailing script, retaining status and standing (making sure that his or her inner hidden <u>shame</u> doesn't become public), and maintaining control of his or her image.[68]

Stonewalling – In simple terms, stonewalling is the act of refusing to communicate with someone. It could be the use of silent treatment, using excuses to avoid communicating, or outright refusing to listen to your needs. Stonewalling

---

68   https://www.psychologytoday.com/us/blog/tech-support/201906/dealing-the-narcissists-smear-campaign Taken 12/12/2023.

can happen in any relationship, but in a relationship with a narcissist it takes on a whole new meaning. Examples may include instances where you were trying to share your thoughts, and they got loud and would not let you talk. They may have even yelled at you and said, "I don't want to hear it!" "Why do you keep bringing it up!" "Don't talk to me" [and yell loudly, "Ahhhh!!!!!"] to overtalk you or loudly cause you to shut down. When this happens, they may accuse you of not communicating effectively.

Trauma Bond - Trauma bonding is a misplaced loyalty where a victim is emotionally bonded with their abuser and finds themselves unable to leave an unhealthy or dangerous relationship. The victim remains loyal to someone who has betrayed them repeatedly. (The Stockholm Syndrome).[69] In the context of narcissistic abuse, trauma bonding explains the victim making excuses for the abuser, downplaying their abuse, or covering their tracks. Trauma bonding involves dopamine, serotonin, adrenaline, oxytocin, and cortisol, all of which play their part in keeping a victim connected to their abuser.[70]

Triangulation – When the narcissist provokes rivalry and jealousy between people, creating triangles of relationships to boost their own ego. Narcissists thrive on chaos. Triangulation involves introducing a third party into a

---

69   https://themindsjournal.com/twenty-common-terms-in-the-world-of-narcissism/

70   https://shecounselling.com.au/narcissism-terminology-your-a-z-guide/ taken 1/22/2024.

conflict or relationship dynamic. The goal is to achieve certain outcomes, such as deflecting tension, creating distractions, or reinforcing the narcissist's sense of superiority.[71]

Trigger(s) – Anything that makes you react or want to react when your needs are not met. It is an emotional response to external events or situations, regardless of your current mood. It could be a subliminal message, passive-aggressive behavior, comments, actions, or inaction in a situation. Narcissists do this to solicit reactions from their victims.

Word salad – Word salad is a verbal assassination. The term "word salad" refers to a circular language tactic used by one individual to ensure that talks never end positively for the other. It is a technique for exerting influence over another person's views or ideas, emotional response, or access to information.

Weaponized incompetence – A passive aggressive psychological dynamic style of behavior where someone avoids or refuses to deliberately perform a task properly by pretending to be incompetent at completing the tasks. The ending result here is usually an unfair division of labor and strained relationship. The decision is conscious and an active form of manipulation so they can live on easy street. See goldbricking too.

Victim blaming – When dealing with narcissism, this form of manipulation happens when the survivor of their abuse or traumatic events become partly or completely

---

71   https://www.bing.com/search?q=narcissist+and+triangulation&form
Taken 2/17/2024.

blamed for their experience. Their response to that experience is downplayed or minimized to almost make the victim feel it was their fault. People who victim blame believe the survivor had control over the situation and could have prevented it by being more careful or behaving better.

Victim Card – Abusing you as they do, narcissists love playing the victim card. This is because they cannot tolerate the reality of the truth you confront them with, as it misaligns with their fantasyland version of themselves. Narcissists use this strategy to gain sympathy from those who they can play with and manipulate later on.

Vulnerabilities - You know those deep, private secrets or insecurities you shared with a narc at the start of your relationship when you were falling in love? Prepare for them all to be used against you later. Narcissists have no shame in throwing your normal human insecurities in your face in efforts to make you hate yourself so that you are further destabilized and, therefore, settle for further abuse. This is the ultimate power trip for a narcissist.[72]

Yes Man – A person who agrees with everything that is said; especially one who endorses or supports without criticism every opinion or proposal of an associate or superior[73]

Zinger – When the narcissists zinger, they insult you in a quick sentence in the middle of a monologue to get it to

72   https://shecounselling.com.au/narcissism-terminology-your-a-z-guide/ taken 1/22/2024.
73   https://www.merriam-webster.com/dictionary/yes-man taken 2/10/2024.

your subconscious. For example, narcissistic parents may say something like, "You never try to organize yourself and that is the biggest reason for your failure.[74]" It is also a quick, witty, or pointed jab as a remark that is used for criticism or insults.

Seeking closure after a breakup is pointless. If someone is telling you through their words and actions that they no longer care enough to keep you, that's all the closure you need.
~Matthew Hussey

---

74   Danish Bashir – Narcissistic Abuse Recovery Professional post.

Life and death are in the power of the tongue. When you speak, you are putting out energy into the atmosphere and creating. You are literally casting a spell. There must also be action accompanying your speaking. However, be careful how you speak to yourself. Both positive and negative words have consequences. It is proven that sound shapes matter. Armed with this information, I know that affirmations and prayers may change the world around us.

About the author

Dr. McKinzie has a passion for helping others. This book is designed to enlighten you about what has been happening to you through your experiences with narcissists.

In order to become the version of me I am today, I had to let the obsolete version of me die. The parts that no longer serve a valued purpose had to be let go of too. It was very painful doing self-reflection, but the inner healing was worth it. I went to therapy; I acknowledged my own role in the situations I had gone through. I found support groups and I even learned to say no. I was under a spell and woke up to reality. I accepted people for who they were and not what I imagined them to be. The hardest part was breaking from being a people-pleaser. The second hardest part was realizing that none of what I was going through was personal. People were merely concerned with maintaining their own interests for themselves. Their character, integrity and influence were all motivators of their behavior, which again, had nothing to do with me personally. Once I found my voice in the room, I used it. I encourage you to do the same. Remember that you are a voice in this world damn it, and you deserve to be heard.

BIBLIOGRAPHY

Allard, Emily Standley. *14 Signs You were raised by a Narcissistic Parent.* https://www.msn.com/en-us/health/other

American Psychiatric Organization. *Diagnostic and statistical manual of mental disorders (DSM-5®).* American Psychiatric Pub; 2013.

Anonymous. *22 Common Examples of Narcissistic Behavior in Men.* From https://toxicties.com/narcissistic-behavior-men/

Andreassen, C. S., et. al. (2017). *The relationship between addictive use of social media, narcissism, and self-esteem: Findings from a large national survey. Addictive behaviors,* 64, 287-293.

Arabia, MA, Shahidi. *5 Attitudes including malicious envy expose malignant Narcissists,* https://psychcentral.com/blog/recovering-narcissist

Aribia, MA, Shahida. *5 Ways Pathologically Envious Narcissists Undermine Your Success.* August 14, 2017 https://psychcentral.com/blog/recovering-narcissist/2017/08/5-ways-pathologically-envious-narcissists-undermine-your-success#1

Asikiwe, Jade. *Overcoming Narcissistic Relationships as an Empath: Breaking the Karmic Cycles of Empaths and Narcissists.* Coppell, TX

Blinkhorn V., et. al. (2015). *The Ultimate Femme Fatale? Narcissism predicts serious and aggressive sexually coercive behavior in females. Personality and Individual Differences,* 87, 219–223.

Carr, Naomi., & Blair, Morgan – Medical reviewer. *Altruistic Narcissist* found on www.mentalhealth.com/.

Jamie Connon, MS, LPC. *What to Expect when you tell a Narcissist "No." How to predict the reactions when you to set limits with a narcissist.* https://www.psychologytoday.com/ March 6, 2023.

Cooks-Campbell, Allaya. *Speaking up for yourself is important – 11 Steps to get it right.* May 20, 2021. https:// www.betterup.com/blog/speaking-up-for-yourself

Cuncic, MA. Arlin. Medically reviewed by Sabrina Romanoff, PsyD. *Can a Narcissist Love?: It's hard to love someone else when you lack empathy.* https://www.verywellmind.com/ can-a-narcissist-love-7112051 taken 12/22/2023.

Davenport, Barrie. *28 Most Glaring Traits of a Female Narcissist.*

https://liveboldandbloom.com/09/emotional-abuse/ female-narcissist September 30, 2023.

Dhawan N, Kunik ME, Oldham J, Coverdale J. *Prevalence, and treatment of narcissistic personality disorder in the community: A systematic review.* Compr Psychiatry [Internet]. 2010;51(4):333–9.

Dowart, Laura. Medical review by Steven Gans, MD. *7 Types of Narcissism: Covert, grandiose, and other types of narcissistic personality disorders.* https://www.verywellhealth. com Update June21, 2023.

Evans, Courtney. *Narcissistic Abuse and Codependency: The complete recovery guide to spot, end, and get over narcissistic and codependent relationships. How to escape from the big trap of the covert narcissist.* Coppell, TX. 2021.

Fleming, LaKeisha. Medically Review by Ivy Kwong, LMFT.   https://www.verywellmind.com/narcissistic-supply December 30, 2023.

Gabbard, G.O., & Crisp-Han, H. (2016). *The Many Faces of Narcissism. World Psychiatry: Official Journal of the World Psychiatric Association* (WPA), 15(2), 115–116. Retrieved from https://doi.org/10.1002/wps.20323.

Green, A., et. al. (2022). *Female narcissism: Assessment, aetiology, and behavioral manifestations. Psychological Reports,* 125(6), 2833-2864.

Grijalva E, Newman DA, Tay L, Donnellan MB, Harms PD, Robins RW, et al. *Gender differences in narcissism: a meta-analytic review.* Psychol Bull. 2015;141(2):261. https://doi.org/10.1037/a0038231

Gupta. Sanjana. Reviewed by Sabrina Romanoff, PsyD. *Use These 10 Phrases to Disarm a Narcissist.* https://www.verywellmind.com/10-phrases-to-disarm-a-narcissis

Hoertel, N., et. al. (2018). *Examining sex differences in DSM-IV-TR narcissistic personality disorder symptom expression using Item Response Theory* (IRT). *Psychiatry research,* 260, 500–507. https://doi.org/10.1016/j.psychres.2017.12.031

SANE factsheet, Narcissistic Personality disorder (NPD) https://www.sane.org/information-and-resources/facts-and-guides/narcissistic-personality-disorder?pdf=yes

Kholghi, Bijan. *What is Monkey Branching? 20 Clear signs and what to do (2025).* http://www.coaching-online.cor/monkey-branching/

Konrath, S. M.M., & Zarins, S. (2016). *The strategic Helper: Narcissism and Prosocial Motives and Behaviors.* *Current Psychology*, 35(2), 182-194. Retrieved from https://doi.org/10.1007/s12144-016-9417-3.

Konrath, S. & Tian, Y. (2017, in press) *Narcissism and Prosocial Behavior.* In Hermann, T., Brunell, A., & Foster, J. (Eds.) Handbook of Trait Narcissism: Key Advances, Research Methods, and Controversies. New York: Springer.

Kowalchyk, M., Palmieri, H., Conte, E., & Wallisch, P. *Narcissism through the lens of performative self-evaluation.* *Personality and Individual Differences*, 2021. 177. Http://doi.org/10.1016/j/paid.2021.110780

Kumar, Surendra. Damage Control. EDUCBA/BLOG. https://www.educba.com/damage-control/

Lawrenz, PsyD. Lori. *Are Narcissists Capable of Love?* https://psychcentral.com/disorders/can-a-narcissist-love#narcissism-and-love taken 2/26/2024

Louise, Rita, PhD. *The Dysfunctional Dance of the Empath and the Narcissist: Create Healthy Relationships by Healing Childhood Trauma.* Library of Congress. First Edition. Dallas, TX.

Mackenzie, Jackson. *Psychopath Free: Recovering from Emotionally Abusive Relationships With Narcissists, Sociopaths, and Other Toxic People.* Burkley, New York, New York. 2015.

Manson, Mark. *Everything is F*cked: A book about hope.* First Edition. HarperCollins publishing., New York, New York. 2019.

Manson, Mark. *The Subtle Art of Not Giving a f*ck. A counterintuitive approach to living a good life.* First Edition. HarperCollins publishing., New York, New York. 2019.

Martinez-Lewi, Linda PhD., LMFT. The Narcissist in Your Life. https://thenarcissistinyourlife.com/cruel-duality-of-the-narcissistic-spouse/ taken 12/31/2023.

Emily Mayfield. *Why are problems never solved with Narcissists?* ttps://www.mindsettherapyonline.com

Mosquera, D. & and Gonzalez, A. *Narcissism as a consequence of trauma and early experience.* European Journal of Trauma and Dissociation Newsletter, 1(4) 2011.

Murphy, Victor. *Highly Sensitive Empaths and Narcissists: The Empath's survival guide to healing from Toxic Relationship. Discover your skills, Understanding your gift, and stop being a victim of Narcissistic Abuse.* USA. 2019.

Nelson, Kate. Fact Checked by Karen Cilli. Verywell Loved: Unpacking What is – and Isn't – Narcissism in a Relationship. Updated February 06, 2022. https://www.verywellmind.com/verywell-loved-unpacking-narcissism

Perry ACC , Elizabeth. *One Life Skill Everybody needs: Learn how to stand up for yourself.* April 5, 2022. https://www.betterup.com/blog/how-to-stand-up-for-yourself

Petho-Robertson, Krisztina. M.Ed., LPC. *How Does a Narcissist Handle Rejection and No Contact?* https://upjourney.com/how-does-a-narcissist-handle-rejection-and-no-contact

Randle, Erica. *Narcissism Terminology| You're A-Z Guide* https://shecounselling.com.au/narcissism-terminology-your-a-z-guide/

Russ, E., et. al. (2008). *Refining the construct of narcissistic personality disorder: Diagnostic criteria and subtypes. American Journal of Psychiatry*, 165(11),1473-1481.

Seamands. David A. *Healing for Damaged Emotions.* Life Journey-Cook Communication Ministries printing. Colorado Springs, CO. 2004.

Stoeber, J. (2014). How Other-Oriented Perfectionism Differs from Self-Oriented and Socially Prescribed Perfectionism. *Journal of Psychopathology and Behavioral Assessment*, 36, 329-338.

The Narcissistic Life. The Narcissist Discard Phase: 3 Signs A final Discard is Coming. https://thenarcissisticlife. com/narcissist-discard/

Vazire, S., et. al. (2008). *Portrait of a narcissist: Manifestations of narcissism in physical appearance. Journal of Research in Personality*, 42(6), 1439-1447.

Volkert J, Gablonski T-C, Rabung S. *Prevalence of personality disorders in the general adult population in Western countries: systematic review and meta-analysis.* Br J Psychiatry. 2018;213(6)   ttps://psychcentral.com/disorders/can-a-narcissist-love#narcissism-and-love:709–15.

Zeigler-Hill, V., et. al (2008). *Narcissistic subtypes and contingent self-esteem: Do all narcissists base their self-esteem on the same domains?. Journal of personality*, 76(4), 753-774.